What to do
When Grief Kidnaps Your Soul

By Rev. Terry Morgan, M.Min.P.S., B.C.E.C.R.

Unless otherwise indicated, all Scripture quotations are from The Holy Bible, English Standard Version® (ESV®), copyright © 2001 by Crossway, a publishing ministry of Good News Publishers. Used by permission. All rights reserved.

Copyright © 2013 Chaplain Terry Morgan
All rights reserved.

DEDICATION

To the love of my life, my wife Phyllis. To the strength of my youth, my son Josh. And to the graceful God worshipper, my daughter Jen. I love you all more than you know. To my friends and fellow workers in Christ who have been called to the ministry of presence – this book is for you. To those who have felt the sting of grief, I pray this book helps you on the journey of grief.

"The heartfelt counsel of a friend is as sweet as perfume and incense." Proverbs 27:9 NLT

CONTENTS

Acknowledgements	vii
Introduction	x

SECTION I

WHEN OUR SOUL IS CRUSHED – DEFINING GRIEF

Chapter 1. Defining Grief	3
Chapter 2. Where is God in my Pain, and Why Does it Matter?	11
Chapter 3. Why Does Grief Hurt so Much	15
Chapter 4. He Holds You in His Hands	23

SECTION II

THE CRY OF OUR SOUL – ENDURING GRIEF

Chapter 5. In Grief's Embrace	31
Chapter 6. Putting a Name on your Grief	39
Chapter 7. Heartache and Pain	45
Chapter 8. Alone in our Suffering?	57

SECTION III

WHEN OUR SOUL FEELS BROKEN – RECOVERING FROM GRIEF

Chapter 9 The Crowd Laughs with you all Year - but only Cries for a Day	69
Chapter 10. If the Devil can't go he Sends a Cynical Christian	75
Chapter 11 A Skunk at a Garden Party	81
Chapter 12 Stop the World I Want Off	87

SECTION IV

HEALING FOR OUR SOUL – COMING OUT THE OTHER SIDE OF THE GRIEF JOURNEY

Chapter 13. A New Path	95
Chapter 14. Practical Suggestions	107
Chapter 15. Memory Hugs	113
Chapter 16. Helping others Through their Grief Journey	117
Appendix A Other Resources	129
Scripture References	131

ACKNOWLEDGMENTS

Many of you have endured such grief that it is unimaginable. It hurts so bad that it is hard to put into words. The title of this book, "When Grief Kidnaps Your Soul", comes from one person's description of the pain of grief. Until a person endures the sting of grief, they cannot grasp the depth of pain one person can endure.

Chaplains meet thousands of you who endure grief across the country every year. Chaplains are often the unsung heroes who get up in the middle of the night leaving their warm bed to respond to calls. These chaplains are often present at the very worst times of individuals lives. Too often it is their role to deliver bad news that will change a life forever. I salute you all my fellow chaplains.

My heart goes out to those who are just beginning the grief journey. My respect and esteem goes to those who have endured the soul tearing pain of grief, and have survived to help others. You who are people helpers have poured yourself into others for so long. Many of these people helpers have been able to express to others what to do to help those in grief. Your contribution is reflected in the pages to follow.

"Blessed are they who mourn, for they shall be comforted."
Matthew 5:4

Chaplain Terry Morgan

INTRODUCTION

We all have felt physical pain. If you live long enough in this world you will experience emotional pain. Most of us will at some point have a deep soul crushing pain that feels like the grief will steal away your soul and hold it for ransom. This pain is so deep it may be very difficult to put into words what you are feeling. No one seems to understand just how bad it hurts making it such a challenge to share with anyone.

People may want you to smile and be happy. They don't want to see you cry. Most people don't know how to deal with someone else's tears. Our culture tries to hide those who are grieving. Society chooses to sanitize our world, and only show what it considers the better side of all of us. Humanity will sometimes reluctantly allow us to express the pain of grief, but only for a short time and preferably in the shadows of a chapel or funeral home. Our world wishes all of us to wear a mask to hide how we are really feeling. The world thinks we should never show the raw emotion under that disguise.

Most people are afraid to allow their sad feelings to show. They don't want to mourn publicly. They may lament on the outside for a time, but only until they are able to seize control of their emotions, cram them down, and put on a "happy face" for those around them.

There may be repercussions for being sad. These repercussions may be real or imagined. We have been taught from a very early age not to cry. People may reject those who grieve and not want to be around them. People will avoid those who mourn for a while because they are afraid of saying the wrong thing that may trigger emotions they are not prepared to deal with. A person who is grieving may see people they know in the grocery store, mysteriously duck down another aisle as if they are trying to avoid them. This is difficult to bear, and hard to understand.

My background as a Chaplain of some twenty years, and over 30 years of ministry has brought me face to face with some of the most devastating grief. I have held people in my arms when they suddenly didn't have the strength to stand. I have looked into the eyes of a family as I have been the bearer of bad news of a death. Chaplain ministry has taken me across the crime scene tape after homicides, suicides, fatal car crashes, severe injuries, and so many other traumatic experiences involving life and death. I have trained chaplains from all over the world how to work with people who are grieving.

This book is all about our grief. It addresses many different kinds of grief, including heart ache from all kinds of loss. We will dare to ask some of the hard questions you may have about grief.

My hope in writing this book is that it will help people through their suffering. It will enlighten the path that countless others have walked before, often in darkness. My prayer is it will bring solace and the comfort of God to a weary soul. When you find yourself at the other end of the path, my hope is you will be able to use some of the principles in this book to help others with their journey.

C.S. Lewis, the beloved Christian author once wrote, **"God whispers in our pleasures, but shouts in our pain."**

SECTION I

WHEN OUR SOUL IS CRUSHED – DEFINING GRIEF

Chapter 1.

Defining Grief

Grief is the pain of loss; it is overwhelming. Grief is hard to describe, and can't be contained – it can tear us apart. Grief is the single most powerful emotion we will ever see. It often manifests itself in anger and disbelief.

Simply knowing that things will eventually get easier to bear can give many people hope to move on. Understanding grief and the grieving process may not alleviate the pain that you are experiencing today. However, recognizing the grief process may help stop the sheer panic of not knowing what is going to happen next. This book goes to great length to explain grief. It describes how to work your way through the grief process to eventually find your self on the other side.

Many people use the words grief and mourning interchangeably. These two terms, though similar have different meanings. Grief is what we feel: the ache in our heart that is so hard to describe. Mourning is the action we take because of our grief such as weeping, sobbing, sighing, and expressing our pain from the loss.

Webster's 1828 English Dictionary gives a more thorough definition of grief than many modern dictionaries. It defines grief as:

> "1. *The pain of mind produced by loss, misfortune, injury or evils of any kind; sorrow; regret. We experience grief when we lose a friend, when we incur loss, when we consider ourselves injured, and by sympathy, we feel grief at the misfortunes of others.*
> *2. The pain of mind occasioned by our own misconduct; sorrow or regret that we have done wrong; pain accompanying*

repentance. We feel grief when we have offended or injured a friend, and the consciousness of having offended the Supreme Being, fills the penitent heart with the most poignant grief."

The word "mourn" is skillfully defined by Mr. Webster in his 1828 dictionary in this way:

1. To express grief or sorrow; to grieve; to be sorrowful. Mourning may be expressed by weeping or audible sounds, or by sobs, sighs or inward silent grief. Abraham came to mourn for Sarah and to weep. Gen 23. Blessed are they that mourn, for they shall be comforted. Mat. 5.
2. To wear the customary habit of sorrow. We mourn in black. Grieve for an hour perhaps, then mourn a year."

Not all grief is the same. There are different degrees and reasons for grief. This book will address many of the different faces of grief including grief from a death, loss of a relationship, and other major losses. There was a time from my childhood when I had a broken heart from losing a favorite toy. I can remember as a preschooler, playing with a little stuffed monkey in our car. My parents, brothers, little sister and I were all going on a road trip to see my grandmother. Grandma lived some twelve hours away from where we lived. Somehow, my little toy monkey flew up in the air and went out the window of our station wagon. I began to cry inconsolably. I was a little child and didn't understand the dangers of stopping on the highway. Even if we could find an off ramp and get turned around, we would probably never find my little stuffed playmate. That is my earliest childhood memory of grief from loss.

Grief is not always caused by the loss from death as we have shown. For a child, the loss of a favorite toy can be heartbreaking. For some people, the loss of a long time job or a career can trigger grief. For others, it may be a betrayal by a friend, or even the death of a pet that causes them to feel as if their soul has been ripped away and torn in two. Not all grief is the same, but all grief is deeply painful.

One thing we know about grief is that everyone grieves differently. We are as unique in this as our fingerprints, or as a snowflake falling from the sky. Some people who are grieving will weep, others may not cry at all. Some people will have a hard time thinking or concentrating. Others may feel numb and not feel anything at all. These are all normal reactions to grief. There are numerous ways people express their grief. However there are some basic reactions that can be observed in every case. These are responses to grief that are common to every person, though they may be stronger and more pronounced in some people. Let's take a look at these and what they mean to us as we are experiencing perhaps the worst time of our entire lives.

There was once a monarch of a small country. He was loved by his people, and had a large family. One of his kids, let's call him Abe for short, grew up to be a very handsome young man. He had movie star good looks, and was, like his father, very well loved by the people of the kingdom. He is described as being very good looking, with a head full of long, gorgeous, curly hair that was the envy of anyone who seen him. Abe was very princely looking.

Unfortunately, the king was often preoccupied with the affairs of the state, and probably was not a very attentive father. He loved his kids, but was often distracted and consumed with taking care of the business of the kingdom and "making a good life" for his family.

Abe was a typical teenager and rebelled against his family. He used his smooth speech, flattering the leaders of the kingdom. He won many people over with his good looks, and his sweet talk. He was able to convince many of the people of the land including some of the faithful followers of his father the king, to rebel against him and make an attempt at overthrowing his kingdom rule. Abe told them he would make a better king, and things would be so much better if only he were king. His Dad didn't see it coming until it was too late. Whether it was the shock of what happened or the love for his son, we can't be sure, but the king fled from his castle to escape the wrath of his son rather than confront him and stop the mutinous overthrow.

Abe and his father both ended up with an army. They fought and went to war against each other. This Dad made it very clear to his army commanders that he wanted his son to be unharmed no matter what. He would attempt to squelch the rebellion, and put an end to this madness, but he was not willing to allow his son to suffer the penalty for his rebellion. The older and wiser monarch eventually began to take back his land. The war was going his way.

One of the very things that made Abe so handsome, his long, thick curly hair, would prove to be his undoing. He was galloping his horse away from a battle when his hair got caught in some low hanging branches. He was left hanging there by his long locks as the horse he was riding ran away without him. One of his father's fighting men found him dangling there. "What good fortune." The soldier must have thought. He thought he would be a hero by doing the monarch a favor and ending the war by killing this rebel leader. He stuck Abe with a javelin and killed him.

The news of Abe's death reached his father. But instead of being happy about the end of the war, he was devastated. The impact of the dreaded news of the death of his beloved though rebellious son caused the monarch deep mourning. He wailed for his dead son. You can almost hear this father's raw emotion as you read his words. King David wept and cried out in anguish, "O my son Absalom—my son, my son Absalom—if only I had died in your place! O Absalom my son, my son!" (II Samuel 18:33b).

GRIEF V.S. MOURNING

Grief is the inability to accept what is inevitable. We will all die. Grief expresses itself in the inability to accept this fact. This is the denial that often comes into play. Our mind is trying to wrap itself around a concept that is so painful – so unimaginable that it can't possibly be true. Our mind tries to protect itself by throwing up a wall of denial that will slowly over time come down.

Mourning is the physical process of healing. Mourning is how we express outwardly what is happening inwardly. It may be exhibited by crying, weeping, and wailing. Sadness, and expressing terms of pain and longing for the missing person is all part of the mourning process. In the not too distant past, a widow or widower would wear black for a period of time to show everyone that came in contact with them that they were in mourning because of a major loss – usually a spouse.

Some people say that mourning lasts until you get your senses back about yourself. There is some truth in that statement. We have learned that mourning is a process of soothing pain that can't be rushed. When a person asks how long is the grieving process, I tell them it takes as long as it takes.

Some people say that after the funeral, you should be "over it". Since the funeral is over, you should now have closure. Unfortunately society often buys into this concept. Mourning and the sense of loss lasts as long as it lasts. It is impossible to put a timetable on it. The one thing we can truly say is one year from now, it won't hurt as bad as it does today. Beyond that there is not much we can say. We can't say it won't still hurt a year from now, but we can say it won't hurt as bad as it does right now.

We as people always seem to want to say, "I know just how you feel." You don't know exactly how someone else feels. Even if you went through something similar, it was not exactly the same. You don't know exactly how they feel, so don't be tempted to say you do. Even if you have experienced a similar loss, you don't know exactly how another person feels. This is one of the worst things you can say, because it always comes across as minimizing their grief and what they are feeling. It doesn't make them feel any better. If you don't know what to say, you are better off not saying anything, and just being present with them as they go through the different stages of grief.

The loss in death is permanent. We don't know how emptiness and loneliness feels until we experience it ourselves. After the funeral, and all the friends and relatives have gone home, the quiet begins to set in. The relationship we had is gone. It is over.

We have learned from experience about pain. We know about pain, and we know that pain hurts. The more pain we have endured in our lifetime the more empathy we can have for another.

Loss invokes feelings of fear and fright. We don't know what to expect. We don't know what to do next. We don't know what is going to happen to us. Children who have lost a parent or older sibling will have feelings of being unsafe. They need to know that they will be taken care of. Anyone who loses a loved one may ask "How will we go on without our loved one?"

Remember, grief shared is grief relieved. Grief bottled up can cause ulcers. It's so important to find a safe person, or better yet, safe people we can talk to and share what is going on inside of us. Crying helps to mend and heal. Being able to share our tears with a trusted friend can go far towards our healing.

OVERCOMING GRIEF

There are some things we can do immediately to begin the process of overcoming grief. The first thing we can do is to take the time to accept death. The sooner we can stop denying the death, the sooner we can begin healing.

Take the time to let go – cry and be vulnerable. Letting go indicates that we are not in control of life. We cannot control everything. Now is the time to cry, and allow ourselves to be emotional.

Don't be in a big hurry to make decisions when you are in the midst of grief. This is especially true immediately after the death of a loved one. Some people will make snap decisions to give away jewelry, cars, or other expensive items that belonged to their loved one. They later regret it and feel like they were taken advantage of. This is the worst time to make a hurried decision.

PUT A NAME ON YOUR GRIEF

It can be very cathartic to put a name on your grief. There is an old saying that goes something like this: "To lose a parent feels like you have lost a part of your past. To lose a spouse feels like you have lost a part of your present. To lose a child feels like you have lost a part of your future." Putting a name on your grief makes it more tangible – to the point you can get a better grasp on what you are feeling.

There was a family who tragically lost their adult son, their only child, to a fatal car crash. Let's call them the Smith family. They were preparing to go to church early one Sunday morning, when they received a knock on the door. Their son had actually been on his way over to have breakfast with them before church. A drunk driver ran through a red light broad-siding his car. He died at the scene. They told me the officer that notified them hugged them and cried with them. Their son had been his friend.

I met the Smith family over dinner at a special event for grieving families. I asked them about their loss, and they told me about their son. It had been over a dozen years since the death. I shared with them about naming their grief and told them, "To lose a child can feel like you have lost part of your future."

As soon as the words were out of my mouth, Mr. Smith suddenly sat up in his chair, and Mrs. Smith began weeping. Mr. Smith looked me in the eye and demanded, "What did you say?!"

I told him again, how losing a son or daughter can feel like losing part of your future. By this time I was very worried I had something that deeply offended them. I was about to apologize. Mr. Smith let out a deep sigh, and fell back in his chair. He told me, "In all these years, we have never been able to explain exactly how we feel. What you said is exactly what we have been feeling but have been unable to express. Thank you so much!"

We went on to talk more about their son. The Smiths told me how everything they had done was for their son. They were financially fairly well off. They had a successful business, and a nice home. Their son was dating a woman, but they had no children. Everything the Smith's owned would one day be passed to their son. With him now dead, they said, they lost their reason for working so hard to make a good future for their son and grandchildren. Putting a name on what they were feeling, even after so many years, was very healing for them. They said it was as if a huge weight had been lifted from their shoulders. It was still painful, but somehow there was a breakthrough for them. For the first time in several years, they both said, they felt like they were "unstuck".

Along with putting a name on our grief, there are some other things that can help. It is important to take the time to feel good; to laugh; and to make new friends. Our loved ones who have passed on would never expect us to be stuck and not feel good about ourselves.

You may be tempted to blame yourself for surviving while your loved one passed away. This may somehow make sense to us even if it isn't logical. If you are feeling this way, take some time and forgive yourself for living on.

Your grief may not involve the death of a loved one. There may be some other reason for your grief. It may be that someone has hurt you, or someone may have passed away before you had a chance to reconcile. Consider if you need to forgive someone. Non-forgiveness is a bitterness that traps people in the past. The person you have not been able to forgive has long since moved on. They may not even realize they did something to hurt or offend you. Even if they did hurt you on purpose, you are the only one trapped – not them. Forgiveness is not the same as pardon. It is a choice – a decision that we make. Forgiveness helps us to look at things in a different way.

Take some time to lean into your faith. There is a difference between facts and faith. Our faith works despite the fact that it is illogical. We believe in something larger than ourselves. We will talk more about how faith can bring us healing in future chapters.

Take the time to give back. We all have some time, energy and effort we can put into others and make a difference for someone else. Getting involved makes life better, and helps us to go on.

Sometimes one of the most healing things we can do for ourselves is to help someone else that is not in a position to ever repay us for our kindness.

Chapter 2.

Where is God in my pain, and Why Does it Matter?

It is not at all unusual to question God when we are grieving. We wonder why God didn't answer our prayers; why He took our loved one; why he didn't intervene and stop something terrible from happening. We question whether God is truly good if He allowed something like this to happen. Some people will have a crisis of faith, and may walk away from God for a while. We may even be angry at God and hold him responsible for some tragic event.

SUSIE'S STORY

There was a particularly tragic and violent death of a little girl. She was a pre-teen picture of innocence. She was popular in school, good at sports, and was the apple of her parent's eye. We will call her Susie (not her real name). It was hot outside, and little Susie called her Mom at work. She always let her Mom know when she arrived home from school so she wouldn't worry. This particular day she wanted to get permission to walk down to the corner store a couple of blocks away for a cold drink and a snack. Her mom gave her permission and told her to give her a quick call when she got back home. Suzie never called. She never returned home. She was kidnapped and brutally raped and murdered by a perverted evil sexual predator.

Susie's parents were obviously devastated. How could something this horrible happen to their innocent little girl? Both of her parents were basically good people. They went to church occasionally, and gave money to charity. They tried to raise their children to be good people. Their whole world had been turned upside down, and now they were getting attention from the community and the media that they never wanted.

Little Susie's parents struggled with what happened. They went from being in a state of despair, to reaching out for answers to the "why" questions. For over a year, they didn't know who murdered their baby. There was little evidence, and few leads. At times they wondered if they would ever know exactly what happened. Susie's Mom embraced her faith, and became a regular at the neighborhood church they had visited occasionally before the death of their daughter. She found comfort in the worship, and people who would love on her and lend her some of their strength. She grew in her faith and leaned heavily into God. Susie's Dad on the other hand, became cold and bitter toward God. His anger towards himself became anger towards God as he blamed Him for his daughter's death. If only God had not allowed this meaningless death, he would have gladly served Him. Not now! Not ever again!

JOHN'S STORY - HOPE IN DESPAIR

John (not his real name) has lived a difficult life. Even his childhood was hard and the circumstances as he grew up would shock many people. He began his career at an early age, and looked forward to what life had in store. Unfortunately, within a few short years after high school he was diagnosed with a progressive debilitating disease. He had dozens of painful surgeries related to the disease. Over the past few decades, it seems like he went from one incredibly challenging trial to the next. He survived cancer, being in a wheelchair for months at a time, and constant pain. He has suffered physically to the point he became suicidal several times – wanting to make the pain stop. Emotionally, he was put through the ringer. Divorce was in his future. He was even falsely accused of a morally vile and despicable crime. John was eventually exonerated of this crime, but the damage was done to his reputation. Many of his friends and acquaintances turned their backs on him, even when he was eventually cleared of the crimes. He tells me that he most relates to Daniel in the Old Testament, who went through such extreme trials, false accusations, and even being cast into the lion's den. But God always took his side. He recently told me, despite another cancer diagnosis, that he clings to God. He said, "Over the years, through trial after trial I have suffered, I have always drawn closer to God through my suffering." He is an inspiration to me.

There is an old saying that the same sun that softens the wax hardens the clay. Some of us will react to grief in such a way that we draw closer to God and lean into Him. Others of us will find ourselves pulling away from God with everything within us. As a matter of fact the same person may react both ways in different situations over the course of a lifetime. One tragedy may drive us away from God, while the next will cause us to rethink our philosophy of religion and embrace God and not want to ever let go.

David was a person in the Bible who experienced more than his fair share of hardship and grief. The Bible gives a pretty complete history of David – this young shepherd boy who would become a king.

David didn't have an ideal childhood. He was the youngest son of a man named Jesse. The prophet Samuel was directed by God to go to Jesse. Samuel went to Jesse and told him that one of his sons would be anointed as the new king. When Samuel asked to see Jesse's sons, he welled up with pride. His boys were tall, strong and handsome. They would be worthy to be a king someday. Unfortunately, he seems to have forgotten all about little David. David was "shooed" off by his other family members to watch the sheep. He was not considered of any importance to the family. Samuel went through each of Jesse's sons, and finally had to ask, "Don't you have another son? Why isn't he here?" David was chosen and anointed to be the future king.

Later in the story, there was a huge battle that went on for many days. The Philistine army had attacked the nation of Israel. Jesse's boys had all gone to fight in the battle – all except David. He was not allowed to go. David eventually was sent to check on his brothers. His brothers ridiculed him, and tried to send him right back home. David surprised everyone when he went into battle against the giant, Goliath, and defeated him. David gained prominence overnight as a war hero and was chosen to become a confidant to King Saul himself.

It seemed like life was finally getting good for David. He went from looking after a bunch of smelly sheep, to living in the king's mansion. But it wasn't to last. King Saul became jealous of David's popularity, and suddenly turned on him and decided to try to kill him.

David's life became one of desperation. He had to flee for his life away from the king, and leave behind his best friend in the world, Saul's own son Jonathan. Jonathan and David had spent time together in the palace. They had played together, hunted together, and even fought side by side. They became closer than brothers. David and Jonathan were the best of friends. It was Jonathan that warned David that his father, Saul, wanted him dead. David had become a fugitive. He felt like the entire world was against him. His days were filled with fear, and grief. He had to keep looking over his shoulder expecting to see the army that King Saul had sent out to kill him. He felt grief from the loss of freedom; the loss from being betrayed by the king and his friends; and even the loss of security he felt while living at home with his family. He was now in constant fear of his life. King Saul was mentally unstable. The Bible says he was tormented by a demon sent from God. Saul hunted for David like he was an animal. On top of that, David had made enemies of other nations while fighting in King Saul's employ, and now they were after him too. David's family found him hiding in a cave. He was afraid for their lives, so he sent them away to a foreign king for protection. This running and hiding from King Saul went on for years.

Eventually, David received word that King Saul and his son Jonathan had been killed. Finally! What a relief! Right? This is probably how most of us would have reacted. But not David. The Bible records that David experienced genuine grief over the death of the King. He was loyal to King Saul despite his mental illness. He never allowed the terrible things that King Saul did to him to make him become bitter. He kept a heart of compassion and respect for the king, because he was God's anointed. On top of that his dearest friend in the world, Jonathan, was also dead.

Anytime David grieved, he would pick up his pen and write. Some of the most beautiful and uplifting Psalms were written by David at the lowest times of his life.

When you are hurting – when you are grieving – when life seems to be more than you can bear, you can turn to the Psalms. The Psalms of David express the heart wrenching grief experiences of one man. An interesting point of the Psalms is how many of them begin by talking about pain and heartache but end up praising God. He describes pain and heart ache so bad that he doesn't know if he can survive it. At times he even asks, "Where is God?" Yet each of these Psalms ends with praise and thanksgiving to God for His faithfulness. These Psalms teach us how we can survive our grief.

Chapter 3.

Why Does Grief Hurt so Much?

It has been said that grief is the price of love. If we didn't love so intensely, we would not grieve so deeply. This penalty is something we are willing to pay for love, though it costs us dearly.

There are many things that will cause us to grieve differently. The gender differences between men and women in itself will cause us to grieve differently. Children grieve differently than adults. A young child will have a very short attention span. They will often cry for a few minutes, then go outside to play. Later they will return to being sad again for a while, followed by more play. The very young have a vivid imagination. They live in a magical fantasy world of their mind. Pre-school children may view death as temporary and reversible. Most children think that death will never come to them, or anyone they know. Elementary school aged children will be able to understand a little more about death. They have a natural curiosity and want to know more about what happened. Anytime you talk to a child about death, you should give them as much information as they can handle. Never lie to them. If you don't tell them the truth of what happened, or don't tell them anything thinking you are protecting them; they will probably make up something far worse than what actually happened.

Some other things that cause us to grieve differently may involve differences in culture, in religious beliefs, and family dynamics. The things that are happening in your life at the time will contribute to how well you cope (or don't cope) with your grief. We are all unique, and everyone grieves differently based on who we are, and our life experiences. However there are many characteristics of grief that are common to all of us.

Grief is more like a journey than an event. It may feel like you are on an emotional roller coaster as you experience a variety of emotions. Early in the grief journey, many people talk about feeling numb and not feeling anything at all. That numbness may turn into a period of seemingly relentless emotional pain. This can be frightening because it is hard to imagine that a person can survive such terrible suffering. It often helps to have a support group to share this pain with. Rest assured you will get better if you don't give up.

As time goes by you may have a couple of good days followed by a really bad one. You may have times of spontaneous crying. This is sometimes accompanied by shortness of breath. Don't think you are having a setback when you have a bad day. This is a normal part of the grief process.

CHARACTERISTICS OF GRIEF

There are certain symptoms that are normally reported by those in grief. There are physical as well as emotional and mental or behavioral characteristics. Here is a brief list of some normal physical reactions you can expect.

- Tightness in the throat making it difficult to talk.
- Unexpected, sometimes uncontrollable crying
- Heaviness in the chest and shoulders.
- All over body aches and pain.
- Light headedness.
- Headaches.
- Deep sighing.
- A mother who has lost an infant may feel aching arms.
- Changes in appetite either decreased or increased.
- Feeling physically exhausted.

Our emotions can feel like they are out of control as we ride the roller coaster up and down. It's important to understand that feeling these emotions is normal. People often talk about the emotions they are having, and then feel guilty because they feel a certain way. They may feel angry and then feel guilty for being angry, or they may be scared, and get mad at themselves for being afraid. Because of this they may even feel like they are losing their mind. You are not going crazy, or losing your mind. These are all normal reactions to grief. Here are some more feelings you may have.

- Feeling numb and not feeling anything at all.
- Feeling as if the loss isn't real – as if it didn't really happen.
- Intense feelings of sadness.
- Depression.
- A deep desire and yearning.
- Anger. This emotion can become intense.
- Guilt.
- Mood swings including a short temper.
- Relief, especially if the grief is for the loss of a loved one who was suffering for a long time, and/or you were the primary care giver.
- Feeling like life has lost its meaning.
- Fear.
- A big upswing in all of these emotions and others can be expected during the holidays, anniversaries, and birthdays.

Loss and grief will cause us to react differently than what is normal for us. Experiencing grief is abnormal for almost all of us. Experiencing something abnormal will cause us to have an abnormal reaction. So to sum up, having an abnormal reaction to an abnormal event is normal. Here are some reactions you may experience.

- Sensing the presence of your loved one. This may include hearing their voice, expecting them to walk in the door, or to be sitting at the table. You may think you see your loved one or see their face.
- Difficulty thinking or concentrating.
- Disorientation.
- Restlessness.

- Difficulty falling asleep, or staying asleep.
- Frequent dreams about a loved one.
- Preoccupation with the loss.
- Questioning of one's faith.
- Stomach upset and other physical symptoms.
- Cold and flu like symptoms – especially immediately following a loss.
- Flare up of pre-existing illnesses.
- Forgetfulness.
- Disorganization.
- Wandering mind.
- Lack of enthusiasm or interest in doing anything.

Whether we believe it or not, we are all created as spiritual beings. We all have a spiritual side, even if we try to ignore or deny it. There are some specific spiritual reactions to grief that are common. Some people who are experiencing grief will seem to draw their strength from their relationship with God, while others will pull away from God. Here is a short list of some of the spiritual reactions to grief that you may experience.

- Questioning faith and beliefs.
- Anger at God.
- Loss of interest in religion or church.
- A feeling of emptiness as if there is no God.
- Search for meaning.
- Pessimism or idealism.
- Embracing of or coming to faith.
- A renewed interest in religion or church.
- Acceptance, forgiveness and compassion – this may be especially but not uniquely where grief is the result of another person(s) e.g. a betrayal by a close friend.

One of the most difficult losses can come from the death of a child. It doesn't matter if the child is young or old. Nothing can prepare a mom or dad for the pain from this loss. We can't fully understand the emptiness and heart ache from the death of a child.

Joseph Bayly, a now deceased Christian author and his wife, lost three children. Their infant was only 18 days old when he died during a surgery. Their five year old died from leukemia, and they lost their eighteen year old to a sledding accident. Bayly was packing some books one day when he noticed the weight limit on the box. He felt inspired by the words and wrote a poem about how he was feeling. Take the time to read his poem a couple of times, and think about the meaning of his words. Here is his poem:

"THIS CARDBOARD BOX" by Joseph Bayly

>Lord
>See it says
>Bursting limit
>100 lbs. per square inch
>The box maker knew
>How much strain
>The box would take
>What weight
>Would crush it
>You are wiser
>Than the box maker
>Maker of my spirit
>My mind
>My body
>Does the box know
>When pressure increases close to
>The limit?
>No
>It knows nothing
>But I know
>When my breaking point
>Is near
>And so I pray
>Maker of my soul
>Determiner of the pressure
>Within
>Upon
>Me

Stop it
Lest I be broken
Or else
Change the pressure rating
Of this fragile container
Of your grace
So that I may bear more.

Joseph Bayly said, "Of all deaths, that of a child is most unnatural and hardest to bear. When a child dies, a part of the parents is buried." This describes the way parents feel whenever a child passes from this life, and this is certainly the way King David must have felt at the loss of his children.

The death of children has occurred in Presidential mansions and average homes like ours. No level of society is immune. King David once lost a seven day old son – a child who was as precious to him as any child to any father who ever lived. His son became seriously ill and lingered between life and death for one week. King David did everything he possibly could to save his son, including pleading with God in prayer. The Bible says he fasted, prayed, and wept all week, but at the end of seven days his precious little boy died.

King David was not a young man. He had lived a difficult life, and was no longer the vibrant young prince he once was. He was a broken man. The years had taken their toll on him. He lived with aches and pains from injuries received long ago, betraying his age. He was once a mighty warrior. This child of his old age was very precious to him. Death is a cruel thief when it steals away our children from us.

There are a few things we can learn from how David grieved. He taught us that it is OK to mourn until we find relief. Grief has to be expressed or it will devour us from the inside out. David didn't try to hide or bury his feelings. He cried openly.

David embraced his faith. He wrote in Psalm 34:18, "The Lord is near to the brokenhearted and saves the crushed in spirit." For those who embrace their faith, or come to faith, there is an unexpected strength that can be found in putting your faith and trust in God. We still grieve, however we don't grieve as those who have no hope. We believe Jesus Christ is the resurrection and the life. Because of Christ we have the hope of being reunited with our loved ones who have died and gone before us.

When King David was told his son had died, he made a statement that has given hope to generations of mothers and fathers who have lost young children. He said as recorded in II Samuel 12:23, "But now he is dead... Can I bring him back again? I shall go to him, but he will not return to me." David knew there was a fixed gulf between this world and the next. His son couldn't return to him, but he would one day go where his son was. David's answer teaches us that our children who die before their parents will be waiting for us in Heaven when we arrive.

When a child dies, he or she takes our hopes, dreams, and expectations with them. They were our future. When they died all of our hopes and dreams may have gone too. It may feel like they have been ripped from us along with our souls. It is a difficult journey. It is a tough truth to accept but we must learn to dream new dreams, and hope new hopes – dreams and hopes that no longer include them.

It is hard for a person experiencing grief to continue functioning at 100%. This is not the time to make major decisions. This is a very vulnerable time and is not a good time to make major life changes such as selling a home, moving, or quitting a job. It's important, if possible, to slow down and allow yourself time to adjust to your loss. It only adds to the loss by making major adjustments to your life too soon after a major loss. We need time to get our senses about us, and get our feet back under us.

A person experiencing extreme grief from the loss of a loved one is very vulnerable to those who would take advantage of them. They may not see a reason to have two cars now; to keep their loved one's expensive jewelry; or other valuables. We as people helpers, chaplains, ministers, and caring friends need to watch out for them during this difficult time. This is especially true the first few days after a death.

Chapter 4.

He Holds You in His Hands

Two dear friends of mine contracted cancer the same year. Both had tumors removed before, had received treatment, and gone into remission earlier in their lives. Russ was given months to live – he had a terminal diagnosis. About the same time, my dear friend Terry was told her cancer had returned, and they needed to treat it aggressively. I spent a lot of time with her and her husband at the hospital, and at their home.

A few months later, Russ had a miracle. The cancer was gone, and he once again went into remission. The doctors even stated it was a miracle. They had no explanation for his recovery.

Terry's cancer spread faster than the doctors could get it into check. The radical treatments were not working. I prayed with her for the last time shortly before she died. It was so difficult to lose her friendship. She had been a trusted advisor, and often offered wisdom and good counsel to me. Her husband is still a dear friend of the family to this day.

**WALKING THROUGH THE VALLEY OF
THE SHADOW OF DEATH**

Russ was one of my best friends, even though he was decades older than I. He always told me I was his mentor, although I think I gained as much if not more from him as he did from me. The man oozed wisdom, compassion, and love for "Father" (his word of affection for God). He loved to sit at the coffee shop at our church and strike up conversations with whoever happened to come in. He often entered into times of ministry and prayer for those he came across. Somehow, people knew he was a person they could confide in, and that he knew how to pray. Russ earned the reputation as being the "Coffee Shop Chaplain".

About a year after his miraculous healing, Russ was diagnosed with a new cancerous growth. The new growth was rare, very aggressive, and deadly. He knew his time was short, and he spent every available moment preparing for his passing, and loving on people.

Russ asked me to arrange a special living memorial for him. He wanted me to conduct a memorial service while he was still alive. This is not an unprecedented request, but it was unusual. He said he probably would not have a funeral service after his death, and he wanted to be able to see all of his friends one more time, and pass along his words of encouragement to them before his passing. How could I say no to this dear man?

We arranged to have special gospel music, various pastors and friends sharing thoughts, a time of open sharing and a short sermon. Russ also managed to get up on a stool and speak his last words to all of those gathered there – about 100 people. There wasn't a dry eye in the place.

Russ shared how he was walking through "the Valley of the Shadow of Death". He had experienced it first hand, the first time he was diagnosed with terminal cancer, and was near death. This second time he was more prepared to go, but still his greatest desire was to have one more chance to be the "coffee shop chaplain" and minister to whomever "Father" would lead his way.

This is an excerpt from the living memorial service we had for Russ:

"Russ shared with me while he was in the hospital his thoughts about Psalm 23, David's Psalm of the Good Shepherd. It talks about walking through the valley of the shadow of death without fear because the Lord is with us. Russ says you can't fully understand this passage until you have walked that path. He thought he was going to die when he went through surgery and treatment for his cancer the first time. He walked that path and he said it was a glorious path. He leaned into the promise that God would never forsake us. As he walked down that path, the presence of the Lord was so sweet.

Russ says that until we walk that path through the valley of the shadow of death there is no testimony. It is still just a promise. He knows that God is there, and will be with him through it all.

Russ has always talked about God as if he really knows him. He calls him "Father". He makes us all feel almost envious of his close relationship with the Lord.

One other thing that should be said about Russ is the example he has lived as a husband and dad. He talks about his wife Pat with such affection. After all these years she is still the love of his life. If there is any regret in his voice, it is in having to leave her behind when he goes home to be with the Lord.

I shared an old poem with Russ a few days ago. It just put me so much in mind of the path that he is walking, and his final destination. This is

"THE OTHER SIDE", by Martha Snell Nicholson

> This isn't death, its glory!
> It isn't dark, it's light;
> It isn't stumbling, groping,
> Or even faith – it's sight.
>
> This isn't grief, it's having
> My last tear wiped away.
> It's sunrise, it's the morning
> Of my eternal day!
>
> It isn't even praying,
> It's speaking face to face,
> It's listening, and it's glimpsing
> The wonders of His grace.
>
> This is the end of pleading
> For strength to bear my pain;
> Not even pain's dark memory

Will ever live again

How did I bear the earth life
Before I came up higher,
Before my soul was granted
It's every deep desire?

Before I knew this rapture
Of meeting face to face
The One who sought me, saved me,
And kept me by His grace!"

Russ stayed long after the service, giving hugs, and advice to everyone at his living memorial. He seemed to be in his element. If it wasn't for the difficulty he had in getting around, you would think that he was not even sick. He seemed to glean strength from the fellowship of his friends and loved ones gathered there in his honor.

It was a short couple of months later that Russ went home to Heaven or "Father's House" as he liked to call it. I still miss my friend. I would not deny him the glory of Heaven, but I sure wish we could have coffee together one more time, and I could glean from his wisdom. Before he passed, I asked him to keep the coffee hot and save a good spot for me. We will have so much to talk about when next we meet again.

WHAT TO EXPECT FROM THE JOURNEY

There was a gentleman who passed away in his eighties. Let's call him Paul. He had been a gospel singer and preacher for much of his life. He became sick, and had some early symptoms of Alzheimer's Disease. His memory started going in the last few weeks of his life, and he would get confused. From time to time he would say, "When can I go home? I'm ready to go home."

His wife of over fifty years would tell him, "Honey, you are home." If he continued saying he wanted to go home she would ask him, "What is your address at home?"

He would give an address for a home where they had not lived in decades. His mind was starting to slip.

A few days before Paul passed away; he had a bad bout and ended up in the hospital. He had some moments of clarity. He told his wife and other family members on two different occasions he had seen a vision. He told them that he had seen Jesus, and that Jesus was laying his hands on his family and praying for them that they would be OK after Paul died. After the second vision of Jesus, Paul looked at his family with tears in his eyes. He said, "If Jesus comes back again, I'm going with him." Paul died a few days later at home. He went peacefully in his sleep.

Paul's wife and family were heartbroken at his death. They were torn, because they knew Paul was where he wanted to be – at home in Heaven with Jesus. But they also knew that they were going to miss him desperately. There were many tears shed at the funeral service for this dear man. But there were also times of joy, and happiness as they gave him a glorious send off to Heaven.

Whether the person who has died is young or old, they will be missed. Some people will say it is easier to lose a loved one who has a long drawn out illness because we have more time to grieve their loss before they die. Grieving is hard work. Most people will shed many tears either when saying goodbye, or in future days when we consider all we have lost.

Grief is a difficult journey that few of us get out of having to experience firsthand. It is not easy and it will change us. No one who has taken the grief journey is ever exactly the same after having taken this trip. Understanding that we will never be exactly the same can bring comfort and peace to those enduring grief's embrace. The Psalmist David was familiar with this and wrote, "Hear my cry, O God, listen to my prayer; from the end of the earth I call to you when my heart is faint. Lead me to the rock that is higher than I, for you have been my refuge, a strong tower against the enemy." Psalm 61:1-3

SECTION II

THE CRY OF OUR SOUL – ENDURING GRIEF

Chapter 5.

In Grief's Embrace

No one can tell you how to grieve or that you are doing it right or wrong. Unfortunately, we often care so much about what other people think that we will try to model the way we mourn to suit other people's opinions. Society has a certain unspoken belief that everyone's grief should fit a certain shaped mold. It's as if they take a big wad of dough – roll it out – and grab their grief shaped cookie cutter. They stamp out a bunch of grief shaped cookies, and say, "There! This is what grief should look like, and if it doesn't fit this mold, there is something wrong with you."

Obviously, there are some normal reactions to grief that most people will experience. A list of common reactions to grief might look something like this: Anger; anxiety; difficulty concentrating or thinking; confusion; weeping (or not crying at all); disbelief; fatigue; fear; frustration; guilt; irritability; feeling isolated; hurting heart; loneliness; numbness; peace; relief; resentment; restlessness; sadness; yearning; and many others. This is only a partial list, but as you can see there are a myriad of normal reactions to grief. There are also many other reactions that are mentioned throughout this book. The point is, grief is hard work – it is painful – and it takes on many different forms unique to every individual.

Grief can seem to distort time. In moments like this one second can seem like an hour. Consider for a moment what can take place in just one second. One small second may make a difference in the outcome of an event. In many of the Olympic competitions, a fraction of a second can be the difference between a gold medal, and not getting a medal at all. One second can be the deciding factor in a winner or a loser. We make many decisions every waking hour of every day. A decision may take a fraction of a second to make. We may not even be consciously aware that we have made a decision. Yet that decision may make an impact on much of the rest of our lives. Sometimes a tragedy can be averted in a decision that takes less than a second. A life may be lost or saved in a mere fraction of time.

Hearing bad news may suddenly seem to cause time to slow down. Our minds are remarkable machines. Our mind can begin working so fast when we are threatened in some way that time seems to slow down to a crawl. We may feel like our feet are stuck to the ground, or as if we are moving through molasses. In reality, time is not slowing down; our mind is just working much faster and more efficiently than normal. Just as in a traumatic incident, such as a car crash, our minds will begin working so fast as to make it seem like time has slowed down. It's a safety measure our brain takes in order to help us survive. There was a time where I was in a car crash that totaled three vehicles. I was making a left hand turn, and someone slammed into me, pushing me into oncoming traffic. When they hit me, my foot came off the brake pedal and I collided with a car coming at me from the opposite direction. I remember trying to lift my foot and apply the brakes to try and stop going into the other lane. My foot wouldn't move, and I couldn't figure out why. It felt like my shoe was stuck to the floor. Witnesses said the whole thing happened in a blink of an eye, but to me I would have said it took at least a minute.

There is an old saying that Humanity lives in a dimension of time and space. We measure time in years, months and weeks - hours, minutes and seconds – But God moves between the seconds. Though we are limited in our world by time and space, God is the creator of time and space and has no such limitations.

To put it in another way, God set up our world and set everything in motion. The Bible says in Genesis 1:1-2, "In the beginning, God created the heavens and the earth. The earth was without form and void, and darkness was over the face of the deep. And the Spirit of God was hovering over the face of the waters." After God created the world, His Spirit hovered, or vibrated, over the face of the earth, creating energy waves, and setting everything into motion. We now measure a year as the equivalent of the earth going around the sun one entire rotation. A month is a measurement of approximately how long it takes for the Moon to travel completely around the Earth. A day is the 24 hour period it takes for the earth to make one entire rotation. But what about the week? The only historical reason for the week is the week of Creation. The Bible says God created the entire universe in just six days. On the seventh day, He rested. The Bible then says the week was to be an example to man throughout history that they should work for six days but rest on the seventh. The seven day week has been recognized throughout written history. It is another evidence for the existence of God, i.e. the belief in Him throughout ancient history. It is also a reminder to us that if God can create this whole universe, set time in motion and populate the earth with creatures great and small – He can take the time to be with you as you go through your time of grief.

PERMISSION TO GRIEVE

Many of us were taught from an early age that we shouldn't cry. If we cried at school growing up, we would be laughed at and called names. As adults, we have come to believe that crying is a bad thing. We don't want to offend others, so we often will not allow ourselves to mourn the way we want to. If we do cry in front of someone, we are quick to apologize to them. We will suppress our emotions. Good or bad, that is the way many of us grew up and learned to control our emotions.

Most of us when in an uncomfortable unfamiliar situation will not act without permission. Being in grief is uncomfortable and unfamiliar for most of us. I want to give you permission to do some of the things you need to do in order to be healthy. There are 12 areas that many experts point to when talking about our grief where we often lack. We may not give ourselves permission to mourn, so we need someone else to give us permission. These 12 permissions are for you. Make them personal and embrace them.

PERMISSION 1:

You have permission to realize your grief is unique. Other people will look at grief differently from the way you do. They have a different set of life experiences that make their grief personal for them. Don't compare yourself to them. Your relationships and experiences; your support system and faith background, and countless other things shape how you will react to loss and how you will grieve that loss.

PERMISSION 2:

You have permission to talk about your grief in your own time. Talking about your loss when you are ready will help with the healing process. It's important to stay in touch with your support system and allow yourself time to grieve and to heal. Seek out the comfort of safe caring friends and relatives who will listen without being judgmental.

PERMISSION 3:

You have permission to walk through a whole list of different emotions. It may feel like you are on a roller coaster ride of different emotions ranging across the whole gamut. This is a normal response to loss and grief. Although it may seem overwhelming at times, you are not losing your mind. The shifting different emotions will ease up given more time.

PERMISSON 4:

You have permission to feel numb and not feel anything at all. Our minds are amazing things. God designed them in such a way as to insulate us from news that is hard to take. Numbness is a normal reaction that insulates us from tragedy. Our brains will process this very difficult information in such a way as to protect us from being completely overwhelmed. It will only allow us to tolerate the maximum of what we can handle, and only accept as much information as it can cope with at a time. It is almost like receiving an anesthesia, or pain killer when we are injured giving us time to heal.

PERMISSION 5:

You have permission to take some down time and do nothing. Grief can be very exhausting work. The feelings of loss and sadness will sap your energy. You may feel very emotionally and physically drained. You will probably not have much appetite. Our bodies can last a long while on very little food, but it is very important that we have enough water.

Drinking water will help our bodies and our mind to function better. You may not feel thirsty, but shedding tears and working through our grief will cause our bodies to lose water. This water needs to be replaced. Realize your physical limitations – take a break – rest and drink lots of water.

PERMISSION 6:

You have permission to experience memory hugs. Memory hugs are those times when you unexpectedly experience grief, tears, sadness or other physical symptoms after a loss. These may happen weeks, months or even years after the event (though they do become less frequent over time). You may be driving down the road and find you need to pull over because you suddenly start crying. Perhaps a familiar song comes on the radio reminding you of a deceased loved one. You may drive past an old favorite hideaway reminding you of something you have lost. Memory hugs can be triggered by a smell, a sound, or even a brief thought.

PERMISSION 7:

You have permission to surround yourself with caring people. It's not always easy to ask people for help. Having people who care about you and understand what you are going through will bring you comfort through this difficult time. Some people are very supportive and will be there when you need them. Others will bring you down and be a drain on your resources. You have permission to not spend your time with those negative people in your life.

PERMISSION 8:

You have permission to use rituals. The funeral or memorial service serves two purposes. It allows you to acknowledge the death of a loved one, and also allows you to share in corporate mourning. Many people today don't want a fuss to be made over them after their death. It may be they don't want a bunch of money to be spent on them for a funeral. The funeral service is not for the dead, but for the living. The funeral service encourages unity in grief and healing for the survivors.

PERMISSION 9:

You have permission to embrace your faith. Our society has a bad habit of saying "two subjects are off limits – religion and politics". Your faith or religion is a very personal thing and you don't need to be embarrassed because you choose to embrace your faith. You can express your faith in whatever way seems appropriate to you. Many people feel hurt and even abandoned by God during times of grief. Being angry at God is a normal part of what many people experience. These feelings will usually pass after a while. Other people will embrace their faith and lean into God during their grief. Some will return to the faith of their youth that they walked away from in adulthood. Seek out non-judgmental people who will allow you to express your faith in whatever way you need to during this time.

PERMISSION 10:

You have permission to ask "Why?" It is common for people to ask why something happened. You may go over the circumstances in your mind trying to figure out why a loss occurred. Some questions have answers, while others don't. Healing can take place in asking the question – not necessarily in getting all the answers.

PERMISSION 11:

You have permission to hang on to your memories. If you are grieving the loss of a loved one, cherish your memories of them. Share those memories with your family and friends. Your memories may make you shed a tear, but they also may make you laugh. Laughter is another sign of how much you loved them. It demonstrates what they meant to you and the good memories you have of them. Don't feel guilty because you laugh during a solemn time. Your loved one would never want you to be stuck in your grief and not enjoy life because of them.

PERMISSION 12:

You have permission to work through your grief and to heal. The wound from a loss cannot heal properly unless it is open. When the wound is uncovered we can openly grieve the loss. Denying the grief, or trying to force down our emotions only makes it more overwhelming. Working through your grief is a process – not an event. It will take time. Be patient, and don't be too hard on yourself. The death of a loved one will change you forever. There is a peace that you can find when you acknowledge this. Many kinds of losses that cause pain and grief will leave you a different person.

Chapter 6.

Putting a name on your grief

It's important to talk about your grief, but it is also important to be choosy about who you share your grief with. Pick just a few people to be completely open and honest with about your feelings. Some people are better than others at listening with empathy. Be selective.

DIFFICULT CONVERSATION OVER DINNER

As time goes by, you can be more selective about how and with whom you express your grief. There are times that are more conducive to open conversations. Sharing a memory and a meal seems to go together very well. There is something very comforting in "breaking bread together".

Family is the primary emotional support for many of us. We have co-workers and friends, but no one knows us like our family. For others, our closest friends take the place of family. The Bible describes some friends as sticking closer than brothers. These friends tend to love us unconditionally. They are also the ones who will be more likely to tell us the truth even when it is painful for us to hear it. We can share our deepest thoughts with these people, and share the brokenness in our spirit. But even our family and closest friends cannot share our grief indefinitely.

It seems all cultures have an unspoken limit on how long is acceptable to continue sharing grief. You may find people avoiding you, or shutting you down if you talk about your grief for too long. This may come as a difficult truth to accept.

Most people will eventually get to where they don't want to grieve anymore. They will grow weary of sharing their grief story. There will come a point where they just don't want to talk about it anymore. Some people will never completely get "over" their grief. This is different from being stuck and not being able to move past the grief to a point where you can function. Before this time the grief may have been constantly present and interfering with your life every day. In those instances where a person feels stuck and is unable to function, it is a good idea to seek professional help to move past the point in their grief where they are stuck.

No one wants to be a burden to their family or friends. However, it is healthier for us to talk about our grief than to cram it down, and not allow anyone to see how we are hurting. There needs to be a healthy balance between sharing enough, and not sharing too much. Here are a few suggestions you can use when talking about your grief:

1. Try not to rehash the same story over and over again. Your pain of loss is a powerful thing. It can be overwhelming. But going over the same sad story and emotions over and over eventually leads to a person actually feeling worse. Try sharing your story from different perspectives. Try to find hope, no matter how small, in your grief. Try to put a specific name on your grief, and also include the hope that begins to break through. You can share something such as "My grief has been overwhelming at times, but other times it is getting easier. I think eventually I will be able to move past this."

2. Be sensitive to your audience. Not everyone is equipped the same way to deal with hearing your grief story. Some people are very empathetic, and

will listen without judgment. Others will have a very hard time just listening and may interrupt you with a way to fix your pain. They mean well and want you to feel better, but don't always realize the way to make you feel better is to just listen. It is very hard to instruct a person on how to help you when you are in the midst of so much pain.

3. Ask for what you need, and then be appreciative. If you really need to talk, tell them so. Let them know it would be really helpful to you if they would allow you to talk about your pain and grief for a while. People are not very good at mind reading. Don't assume they know what you are thinking. After sharing, be sure to thank them for listening. You can observe how they handled listening to your story to see if they would be a safe person to trust with more, or if you need to be selective about what you share.

4. Seek help from grief counselors and/or a support group. Both grief counselors and support groups can hear your story and will be able to offer strength. You can join a support group of people who are very similar to you. There are support groups for grieving fathers; parents who have lost children; those who have lost a loved one to suicide, cancer, homicide, etc. There is something very healing in knowing other people have gone through something very similar to what you have experienced. Support groups also tend to be made up of a mix of people who are at different places along their grief journey. There will be some who have recently gone through a loss, as well as those who have survived for a while, and can help those who are just starting the process.

Remember, most of us can talk more than one person can listen. Don't flood one person with everything going on. Find several compassionate listeners that will give you the grace and the time you need to talk about your grief without them feeling overwhelmed.

IDENTIFYING OUR GRIEF

It is not easy to put a name on our grief. We may need help from our friends and family to identify exactly what we are feeling. There is something powerful in naming our grief. It seems to help us process better if we know what it is we are feeling.

Lao Tzu was an ancient Chinese philosopher. He is quoted as once saying, "Being deeply loved by someone gives you strength, while loving someone deeply gives you courage." The deep love we feel for someone can drive us to extreme measures to protect them – even to laying down our lives for them. No wonder we say it feels like someone has kidnapped our soul when we lose someone we love so deeply.

So what do we do to show we are grieving a loss? Perhaps a better question would be, "How should we mourn?" Did our ancestors have the right idea, wearing black for a year? Other cultures wail, throw ashes in the air, and beat their chests. I have seen people scream, run around, and even slam their fists into walls. Other grieving individuals become very quiet and reserved, virtually shutting down all emotion. I recall responding to the home of one family who lost a son to an accidental gun discharge. They wept and wailed all night. Early in the morning, the wife excused herself, showered, and changed into her work clothes. She went off to her job. She said her culture taught that her son's spirit would be stuck and not be able to move on if she continued to mourn. I worked with this family off and on for about a month, including doing the funeral service for their son. I never saw this woman cry again after this night of weeping.

King David suffered a great deal of loss. At different points in his life he suffered from losing a baby; losing an adult child; being betrayed by his closest friends; he lost his home and security more than once; and there was a time his whole family was kidnapped by terrorists and he was blamed for it. David was a prolific writer. In Psalm 6 he pours out his heart in anguish. This is one of his psalms where he describes suffering in terrifying, gut-wrenching detail. Here is the text of Psalm 6 from the English Standard Version (ESV).

Psalm 6: "O Lord, rebuke me not in your anger, nor discipline me in your wrath. Be gracious to me, O Lord, for I am languishing; heal me, O Lord, for my bones are troubled. My soul also is greatly troubled. But you, O Lord—how long? Turn, O Lord, deliver my life; save me for the sake of your steadfast love. For in death there is no remembrance of you; in Sheol who will give you praise? I am weary with my moaning; every night I flood my bed with tears; I drench my couch with my weeping. My eye wastes away because of grief; it grows weak because of all my foes. Depart from me, all you workers of evil, for the Lord has heard the sound of my weeping. The Lord has heard my plea; the Lord accepts my prayer. All my enemies shall be ashamed and greatly troubled; they shall turn back and be put to shame in a moment.

Psalm 6 seems to be the quintessential psalm for the person enduring grief and suffering. David seems to feel our pain in this Psalm along with us. It has been described as the psalm of those in the hospital when the painkillers are not enough – the up all night crying out in desperation psalm – the psalm for the one who is brokenhearted. If you don't know how you should mourn, perhaps King David's example in Psalm 6 will help.

Chapter 7.

Heartache and pain

There are many kinds of loss, and grief from that loss. The most common grief that everyone has to endure at some point in their lives is the loss of a loved one to death. This grief has been written about by poets; talked about by philosophers; and taught by theologians. It is recorded and described in the Bible. The heart ache and pain from losing a loved one has led to the most agonizing grief a person will endure and sometimes lasts an entire life time. Much of this book is dedicated to addressing this specific kind of grief. However in this chapter we will look at grief caused by other kinds of loss.

GRIEF FROM LOSS OF A JOB

Grief can be experienced after any kind of loss. There is a certain amount of grief experienced when losing a job – even if you hated where you worked. Most everyone has experienced losing a job at some time or another, and it is almost always a painful experience. You may have done something to deserve being fired, or you may have been laid off due to cut backs. You may have lost your job due to something not your fault at all. You could have hated your position or loved it. The circumstances surrounding being let go from your work will determine the depths and levels of grief you may endure at its termination.

If you lost a position you hated, the transition to being without work may not be nearly as painful as it would be if you loved your job. But, if you have no savings, and have little opportunity to quickly find other work it may make things much more difficult.

It is possible to hate your job, but still have an intense feeling of loss especially if you worked there for a long period of time. This grief may come as totally unexpected. It is normal to cry, be angry and upset after losing a job. You may be afraid of being unemployed or you may feel like you failed when you lose a job. There are a variety of reasons you may feel a sense of loss.

It is important to not spend too much time in mourning the loss of a job. It is understandably painful, but the sooner you get back out looking for work, the sooner you can take advantage of new opportunities and work through this kind of loss. There are many resources to help you find another job. There are books, articles, and blogs about all aspects of the job hunt. Suffice it to say here that the loss will get easier when you are able to secure another job. It has been my experience that the next job is often better than the last and you soon forget the loss of the previous employer.

LOSS OF A RELATIONSHIP - DIVORCE

There is another kind of loss that can also be extremely painful and long-lasting. This loss has sometimes been described as equal to - or even worse than losing a loved one to death. Some people say with a divorce, there is not the same sense of closure as with a death. Grief can be very strong when it is caused by the loss of a relationship. You may feel betrayed, and deeply hurt, especially if there was an affair. Divorce will inevitably be deeply hurtful for both individuals involved regardless of intentions. If there are children involved they will also be deeply hurt despite the best efforts of the parents to insulate them.

When a man and woman are married, the Bible says they are joined together and they become one flesh. This concept is laid out in the book of Genesis (Genesis 2:24, "Therefore a man shall leave his father and his mother and hold fast to his wife, and they shall become one flesh.) and repeated in several places in the New Testament. When God created Adam and Eve, his intention was that they would complement each other and be part of a whole. Just like if you take a loaf of bread and cut it in half. You now have two halves of the same loaf – not two separate loaves. When a man and woman are married, they are no longer considered two individuals, but one married couple. When they have children, their offspring are a product of the union, and are part of the man and part of the woman.

When divorce splits the union of a man and woman it is as if they are being torn asunder. The whole family suffers. There are often extenuating circumstances that lead to the divorce. It may be an illicit affair on one or both partner's part. There may be financial difficulties that lead to heated arguments. People talk about "falling out of love" but it is rare that there is not some circumstance that fed the desire to separate. There is a unique intimacy that comes with being married. Divorce is so painful in part because it is a process of ripping two souls apart that have been joined together. The intimacy is gone. In its place are pain, heartache, and grief.

There are no easy answers to getting help after divorce. The grief will be painful. There is no getting around that. There are good support groups that can be beneficial. Counseling is also a very good idea. With counseling, it may be possible to reconcile the relationship (hopefully before the divorce). Even some of the most irreconcilable differences can be overcome if both parties are willing to try. Love can cover a multitude of shortcomings. However, not all separations or divorce end in reconciliation and I don't want to give false hope.

LOSS OF A RELATIONSHIP - BETRAYAL

Betrayal by its very nature is always committed by someone very close to us. Being betrayed, whether by a dear friend, or a spouse, is not something easy to bear. It can feel like you are being ripped apart. If you have ever been betrayed you know the ensuing pain that results from it. It would not hurt nearly as much if the action was done by someone who wasn't so close to us. Jesus himself was betrayed by a close friend. He was led away, beaten and crucified because of the betrayal of one of his own disciples. Not only that, but he actually told the soldiers that he would kiss Jesus so there would be no mistaking he was the one they wanted. This was one of the bitterest kisses in all of history.

King David also experienced betrayal by a friend. One of King David's sons was named Absalom. Absalom was a handsome man and very popular. He decided he wanted to be king in his father's place, and led a revolt against him (see chapter 1). David had a trusted friend and advisor named Ahithophel. Ahithophel joined the conspiracy against David. His betrayal directly led to the death of two other men whom David loved.

The story of David's betrayal is a sad one. His onetime close friend and confidante Ahithophel actually asked David's son Absalom for a small army to chase after David with the intention of killing him. He thought this would put him in good graces with the "new king." But Absalom denied him permission. Ahithophel felt ashamed, perhaps partially for betraying his friend. Maybe he knew if David did return to the throne he would be tried for treason and put to death. We don't know what was going through his mind. But we do know he went home so ashamed that he committed suicide.

King David later wrote from his heart about the betrayal by his friend Ahithophel. Over in Psalm 41:9, he wrote, "Even my close friend in whom I trusted, who ate my bread, has lifted his heel against me." It should be noted that one of the greatest insults in the Middle East is to turn the bottom of your shoe or foot to someone. David was saying, not only did his close friend betray him, but he threw the betrayal in his face with the ultimate insult.

Jesus Christ's betrayer was also a friend who ate regularly at his table. Judas, perhaps impatient for something big to happen, or perhaps just out of greed and avarice went to some of Jesus' enemies. The religious leaders at the time wanted Jesus dead. Judas went to them and negotiated the cost of betraying his friend. He asked for 30 pieces of silver. This was ironically, the lowest price paid for a slave in Jerusalem at that time. So for the price of a slave, he would sell his friend and betray him.

Judas knew that Jesus had a habit of going to a garden just outside of town after the evening meal. It held a quiet solitude and comfortable beauty. He may have offered to point out Jesus to the soldiers, but they wanted more for their money. Judas would betray Jesus with a kiss. He did this, and Jesus asked him, "Judas, are you betraying me with a kiss?" This was like a slap in the face.

Later Judas must have had time to think about what he had done. Maybe he thought the other eleven disciples would figure it out and come after him with a sword and bring retribution on his head. Or more likely the shame of what he had done was more than he could bear. He tried to return the money, but it was too late. The Bible tells us that Judas was ashamed, and just like Ahithophel, he went out and hung himself.

Dale Carnegie was a great lecturer. He wrote a best-selling book called, "How to Win Friends and Influence People." Carnegie talks about how he once visited Yellowstone Park. He noticed that Grizzly bears would show up at the park looking to find morsels in the garbage. They would never allow any of the other animals to forage alongside them. Any other animal that dared to approach would either be ran off, or killed. There was one exception. There was a "little critter" weighing no more than about 18 pounds. This creature could dig around in the garbage next to the grizzly bear without fear of being harassed. What courageous little animal didn't fear the grizzly? Only the little black and white striped skunk.

Skunks can sometimes be found eating right next to a bear. A Grizzly Bear can fight and beat almost any other animal in the United States. Carnegie talked about how the grizzly must resent the little skunk, and if challenged, could easily kill it without a second thought. There is no doubt that the grizzly bear resented the intrusion on his territory. But he didn't raise a paw to the skunk. The natural question is, "Why not?" The simple answer is the bear knew the high cost of getting even.

Bitterness is something that will eat away at the strongest person. Like a slow acting poison, bitterness will affect every area of a person's life. It is like an acid eating away at the soul. But there is an antidote for this poison – a certain cure for this cancer of the soul. It is forgiveness. Forgiving a person who betrays you is not always easy. They may not deserve it, and may never seek your forgiveness. But forgiveness is more for you than the other person. Forgiving a person doesn't mean you forget what they did, or that you will ever trust them again, but you no longer hold on to it. By forgiving, you are giving up any right to retaliation. You are releasing someone from the wrong they have done to you – but in effect you are releasing yourself. The grizzly bear knew that he could beat the skunk, but would have to pay consequences for a long time for his action. In much the same way, holding on to bitterness and looking for revenge does more harm to you than it does to the one who "sold you for 30 pieces of silver."

GRIEF FROM THE LOSS OF A REPUTATION

We are all human. Sometimes we have such a big, public failure we lose the confidence of all who love us. Our reputation is soiled, and it may be beyond repair. We may condemn ourselves and find ourselves in such a low morale that we think we can never be restored. Fortunately, we have many examples from scriptures that show even if we do something horrendous, we can be forgiven and eventually have an impact again in our chosen field. One example that comes to mind is that of the Apostle Peter. Peter had a volatile personality. He stooped so low as to deny that he even knew Jesus Christ three times. But later, Jesus Christ himself told Peter he would use him to build His Church. In fact, Peter became a leader in the church of Jerusalem, and preached the gospel everywhere he went.

It may be that your reputation has been destroyed by a false rumor, or an ugly accusation. There are ministers who have lost their position within their church because of a person who for whatever reason decided to go after them and purposely damage their reputation. They use false accusations, division, and gossip as weapons. Their only goal seems to be to take down the pastor and cause them to lose their position in the church. I have talked to many pastors who have experienced this at least once in their career. This happened to me a few years ago, and it was one of the most painful things I have ever been through in my life. Unfortunately this happens far more often than most people realize. This phenomenon of attacking ministers with false accusations, and gossip has become so common in recent years that they have actually coined a term for it. They call such people who purposely try to harm and remove ministers from their churches "clergy killers."

Do you remember the story of Joseph in the Bible? Joseph was a young man who had big, God inspired dreams. Joseph was part of a big family, and he was next to the youngest. When he started sharing the dreams he had, his older brothers became angry and bitter against him. They developed such a hatred for him that they were going to kill him. Eventually, instead of just killing him, they took and sold him into slavery. They told his father that some wild animal must have killed him, and gave them a bloody coat that belonged to him to back up their tale. Joseph's story didn't end there.

Joseph ended up as a servant in the household of a powerful Egyptian named Potiphar. He was treated well, and worked hard without complaining. Joseph did such a good job for his Egyptian master that he was promoted to the chief of his household. Joseph's hard work, not to mention his rugged good looking features, didn't go unnoticed. Potiphar's wife took an interest in this young man. She repeatedly tried to seduce him, but Joseph would have none of it. He was a person of strong faith in God, and knew that adultery was a sinful act.

One day, Potiphar had to go out of town on a trip. He left Joseph in charge. Potiphar's wife thought this was her opportunity. Her husband was gone for a few days, so now surely Joseph wouldn't refuse her passions. She sent all of the other servants out of the house to do various tasks, and then called Joseph up to her room. She made her move on Joseph. She insisted that he was her servant and he was to sleep with her, and she would not accept a refusal. Joseph took off. He tried to run from her, and she literally grabbed him, pulling off his outer coat.

Potiphar's wife was ashamed, embarrassed, and furious at Joseph for refusing her advancements. When Potiphar returned, she cried "rape" and showed him Joseph's coat as proof. Joseph's reputation had been destroyed – his employer and friends no longer trusted him – and he was thrown into prison.

Joseph later was not only released, but he was promoted to the second highest position in all of Egypt, second only to the Pharaoh. It's a wonderful story about how a person, who did no wrong, can be lied about – falsely accused and condemned and can eventually be exonerated and have everything restored to them.

The point is, not every person who loses their reputation deserves it. You may be a person who has lost everything over a false accusation. You may have every reason to hate the people who accused you, just like Joseph. Joseph eventually met his brothers again, and he was able to forgive all of them for what they did to him.

If you are guilty of what you are accused of, you may be trying to justify your actions. You need to repent of your actions, and seek forgiveness. But you also may need to forgive those who caught you and handed you over to be punished.

A loss of reputation, especially for a man, can be a devastating loss. This doesn't mean that a woman won't feel grief if it happens to them, but a man relates his career to his entire life. There is a deep grief that accompanies his loss of reputation. When you ask a man who he is, they will almost always tell you their name and then talk about what they do for a living. A counselor once asked me, "Who are you outside of your job?" It took me a week of soul searching to answer that question without referring to my work.

Some people like to say that grief is like an onion. Every time you peel away a layer of grief, it can bring tears to your eyes, and you find another layer. Over a lifetime, we experience a lot of grief from losses we suffer. But if you keep peeling back the layers of onion, you eventually end up with nothing. Someone said that grief is more like an artichoke. Each layer of an artichoke has a thorn on the end. If you're not careful, it can stab you. But when you finish peeling back all the layers you will find the heart of an artichoke. That is the way we are. If you keep peeling back the layers of grief, of pain, and longing, you eventually find our heart.

MORAL INJURY

Those coming back from war often have physical injuries. Some may be missing limbs, or have visible wounds and disabilities. More often, there are invisible wounds that have a devastating effect on our young men and women coming home after seeing battle. PTSD (Post Traumatic Stress Disorder) and TBI (Traumatic Brain Injury) are common ailments afflicting our troops. There is another silent killer out there however that is just recently getting attention called Moral Injury. Moral Injury is the result of having to make difficult moral choices under extreme conditions, e.g. having to take a life. Moral Injury involves experiencing morally anguishing actions or duties; witnessing immoral acts; or taking an action that profoundly challenges a person's moral conscience. It involves going against who you are and the moral values that you strongly identify with. For a person of faith it involves going against everything you believe in.

It is generally supposed that there are three pieces, or parts to the cause of Moral Injury. 1. There has been a betrayal of a person's moral code of what is right. 2. This is done by someone holding legitimate authority (such as a ranking officer in the military), or by the service member themselves. 3. It takes place in an extreme and significant or risky situation. The person may be responsible for, or failing to prevent the event; bearing witness to it; or learning about acts that violate their deeply held faith, moral beliefs and expectations.

The symptoms of Moral Injury are similar to and usually accompany PTSD and/or TBI. There is a strong sense of guilt, depression or worry involved with Moral Injury that can make the symptoms of PTSD and TBI much worse. There may be a great deal of survival guilt, and shame.

Moral Injury can cause a person to lose their trust in the Holy. They may also experience a lack of confidence in the Community of Faith (their church family), the government or law enforcement, family and friends. It is as if the person has a shattered self image. They have lost the person they thought they were. The person may feel like they have had an encounter with true evil – externally, internally, or both. One young veteran said it feels as if his soul is now separated from his body.

The person suffering Moral Injury will feel an agony from the atrocity they experienced. There is such a sense of loss that it is difficult for a person who has not experienced this for themselves to imagine. Their view of the ultimate meaning in life has been stripped away. If they were a person of faith, that faith may have been challenged to the point that they no longer believe: or their faith may have been dramatically altered with no clear path how to repair and rebuild the foundation of their faith. Addressing the moral injury can make symptoms from PTSD and TBI manageable.

CANDY COVERED HAND GRENADES

Words can hurt. Words can also build up and give life. There was a person who said a long time ago that "sticks and stones can break my bones, but words will never hurt me." I think that person either had never experienced the deep wounds that can be inflicted by another person's words or they had been so hurt that this was their only defense – posturing as if they had not been hurt. Sometimes people can give what sound like well meaning words that actually are designed to hurt us more. They may be intentionally hurtful, but more often they are given as a way to express their condolence for our loss but in a way that only makes themselves feel better. Those that do not intentionally hurt with their words, usually do so out of ignorance, not malice.

All of the different kinds of loss mentioned in this chapter have one thing in common. They all involve other people and relationships in our lives. But whether the grief comes from the loss of a job or a relationship: if it comes from a betrayal or even the loss of our reputation, we must not allow ourselves to become resentful. It is very easy for us to become bitter against the person who hurt us. We may even become angry and bitter against God. Unforgiveness will always lead to bitterness. Bitterness can begin so small it is almost invisible. Over time it can take root and begin to grow. Eventually bitterness, if not dealt with, will grow until it takes over our lives.

Hebrews 12:15 talks about how bitterness can grow. It reads, "See to it that no one fails to obtain the grace of God; that no root of bitterness" springs up and causes trouble, and by it many become defiled;" Becoming bitter can happen to anyone. But bitterness only leads to more pain and grief.

Corrie Ten Boom has always been one of my personal heroes. She was a Christian woman who was part of a German family during WWII. She and her family were arrested for harboring and helping the Jews escape from Nazi Germany. She was placed in a horrific concentration camp, where her sister eventually died in her arms.

Corrie talked about how she could not forget the wrong that had been done to her and her family by the Nazi soldiers. Through the Grace of God she was eventually able to forgive them, but she kept reviewing the incidents in her mind. She had a lot of trouble sleeping because of it.

Finally, Corrie cried out to God for help in putting the problem to rest. She journaled what happened after that. She tells of how help came in the form of a kindly Lutheran pastor. He talked to her about the bell up in the old church tower. The bell was rung by someone pulling down hard on the rope. He explained how, after the rope is released, the bell will keep ringing several times. The bell will toll very loud at first, but each time it rings it will be a little softer until it finally stops. When we forgive, it is as if we finally remove our hand from the rope. If we have been "tugging at our grievances" for a long time, we should not be surprised if the old thoughts keep coming for a while. The old bell is slowing down, but it may "ding – dong" for a while longer.

Corrie talked about this story, telling how the old pastor was right. She was no longer surprised by the angry, hurtful thoughts. But she was able to reassure herself that these were just dings and dongs from the old bell chiming as it slowed down. Without her continuing to "pull the rope" by wallowing in her bitter angry feelings, they came less and less often and somehow lost the power they once had over her.

TIDBITS ABOUT FORGIVENESS

- Forgiving doesn't mean you forget. You can be sincere in your forgiveness even if you remember.

- You are not overlooking people's faults when you forgive them. You are only able to forgive them because you DO hold them accountable for what they did.

- Forgiveness deals with our emotional response. It is not the same as pardoning a person for their actions. Only God or a judge can offer a pardon.

- Forgiveness is an act of the will. It lifts the weight from off our shoulders.

- Forgiveness offers a chance at reconciliation. It can heal a broken relationship.

- Forgiveness can unshackle us. The person who caused the offense may not know that they did anything to us – they may have long forgotten – or they may not even care. When we refuse to forgive, we are the ones being held in bondage by the person who did the offense to us, not the other way around.

- The alternative to forgiving is a life filled with hurt, bitterness, and resentment. It is filled with a poison that destroys other relationships, and causes us to not trust even those who have done nothing to lose our trust. It creates a pattern that may stick with us the rest of our lives. It is a cynical acidic poison eating away at our souls that eventually kills its owner.

Chapter 8.

Alone in our suffering?

It is not unusual or even inappropriate for us to question God during times of despair and deep grief. Even people who consider themselves people of strong faith may be moved to ask such questions. It doesn't mean we are abandoning our faith – we are simply crying out from the anguish in our soul. We are expressing a pain that is indescribable, and demanding answers to questions that may have no answer this side of Heaven.

Have you ever asked these kinds of questions?

"Did God allow my loved one to die?

I thought God was supposed to be there for us and answer our prayers?

What was God thinking when he allowed me to lose everything?

Is He really out there?

Does God really exist?"

These are all legitimate questions. We have all questioned God at one time or another if we are honest with ourselves. Maybe we felt guilty for questioning Him. Or maybe we were so angry and hurt we just didn't care for a while. We may ask where is He and why did He allow this to happen?

God has really big shoulders. He can handle our questions. He is here now, and will be here when we finish asking our questions ready to embrace us with open arms. David questioned God on many occasions, crying out to Him for answers. David expresses his hurt, fear and frustration without apologizing for it.

An African proverb says, "The one who asks questions doesn't lose his way."

WHERE IS GOD IN MY SUFFERING?

Our grief can cause us to feel lonely and afraid. We may feel like God has abandoned us. The poem, "Footprints in the Sand", by Carolyn Joyce Carty seems to capture what we may feel and puts this question into words for us.

"FOOTPRINTS IN THE SAND" by Mary Stevenson

One night a man had a dream. He dreamed
he was walking along the beach with the LORD.

Across the sky flashed scenes from his life.
For each scene he noticed two set of
footprints in the sand: one belonging
to him, and the other to the LORD.

When the last scene of his life flashed before him,
he looked back at the footprints in the sand.

He noticed that many times along the path of
His life there was only one set of footprints.

He also noticed that it happened at the very
Lowest and saddest times in his life.

This really bothered him and he
questioned the Lord about it:

"LORD, you said that once I decided to follow
you, you'd walk with me all the way.
But I have noticed that during the most

troublesome times in my life,
there is only one set of footprints.
I don't understand why when
I needed you most you would leave me."

The LORD replied:

"My son, my precious child,
I love you and I would never leave you,
During your times of trial and suffering,
when you see only one set of footprints,
it was then that I carried you."

We may question God, just as the person in the poem, without losing our faith in God. We can trust God even when we don't understand Him. God continues to be at our side, and at those times when we have no strength to take another step – he carries us.

God understands us better than we know ourselves. He knows all about pain and suffering. He knows the pain of children who rebel, and turn their back on their family. He knows how we as God's children, harm each other, abuse His creation, and pretty much neglect Him. He also knows the heart wrenching pain of having a son be despised, rejected, betrayed, and eventually killed experiencing a long and painful death.

God is all powerful. He created the universe. He made humanity in his own image. He could have made us to obey his every wish. But instead he chose not to make a bunch of automatons. He gave us free will and the ability to choose to serve Him or not. Unfortunately, given the choice to obey God or not, man chose to rebel against God and eat the forbidden fruit in the Garden of Eden. This led to all kinds of unforeseen trouble for us. The end result is death. Romans 5:12 tells us, "Therefore, just as sin came into the world through one man, and death through sin, and so death spread to all men because all sinned—"

God is omnipotent, meaning He is all powerful, and omniscient or all-knowing. There is nothing He could not do if He so chose to. He made the universe by simply speaking the word. Although God is all powerful, possessing all knowledge, with the ability to be everywhere at once, He is also a gentleman. God will not force His will on anyone. We all have free choice and free will. But since we do all have free will, there is no guarantee that the choices we make will be the right ones or the best for us. Sin is a powerful agent in our lives. We live in a fallen world. Death is ultimately a result of original sin, and humanity is corrupt because of sin. Some people give themselves totally over to their own lusts, and sin, and do harm to other people.

The power of sin leads us to make bad choices. It affects our every decision and the effect of sin causes the whole earth to spiral down into chaos. We see the affects of sin every day. All you have to do is turn on the news.

The Bible promises that someday Jesus Christ will return to Earth and establish a kingdom of peace. But that day is still sometime in the future. Meanwhile we have to continue on in this fallen world.

When I was growing up, my parents put a little plaque on the wall in our living room. I can remember staring at that little plaque as a small boy, for long minutes at a time. I would sit and try to fathom what it meant. As an adult it has become one of my favorite promises from the Bible. The verse on that plaque from my childhood can be found in Hebrews 13:5. It says, ""I will never leave you nor forsake you."

God promises that He will always be with us. There was a popular Country and Western song from several decades ago that simply said, "I beg your pardon, I never promised you a rose garden." The Bible says that we should expect trials and tribulations and treacherous times. God never promised that we would never face pain. The pain we suffer can be directly attributed to sin. Sometimes it is caused by the sin influenced decisions we or others make. Sometimes it is a direct result of living in a fallen world where sin has taken its toll. The good news is that God has promised that through it all, He will be there with us if we let Him. We can lean into Him. He is strong enough to hold us and never let us go.

King David was known as a "man after God's own heart" (see Acts 13:22, 1 Samuel 13:14). Yet, even David asked where is God when I am suffering? He wrote a Psalm describing his pain. He said in Psalm 22:1-2, " My God, my God, why have you forsaken me? Why are you so far from saving me, from the words of my groaning? O my God, I cry by day, but you do not answer and by night, but I find no rest." Have you ever felt that way?

It felt to David as if God had abandoned him. Have you ever prayed and felt like your prayers only made it to the roof? It may have felt like the heavens were made of brass and there was no way for your prayers to get through. David was in a miserable state thinking God had led him all this time – through many battles, being chased through the desert by an insane king, and even to the throne – only to abandon him now. That would be a sad ending to Psalm 22. Thankfully that was not the end of a poignant and beautiful passage. Verses 3-5 says: "Yet you are holy, enthroned on the praises of Israel. In you our fathers trusted; they trusted, and you delivered them. To you they cried and were rescued; in you they trusted and were not put to shame." These verses are a reminder that God had helped him and the kingdom of Israel in the past. He knew that God could help him now. Even though it didn't feel like it, God was there and did hear his prayers. He goes on in this Psalm to praise God for his deliverance, and that those who seek the Lord will find Him. He knew, despite how he was feeling at the moment, that God was there and would walk with him through his grief.

God never intended for us to endure pain and grief all alone. He is with us, but He also made us in such a way that we have a deep need for human companionship. Even those who would be considered "loners" will bloom and grow when touched by human kindness.

There was a man who gave a lecture I attended. He had been held as a political prisoner in a communist dungeon. He talked about his suffering – the daily beatings – and the desperate conditions he endured for over a decade. He eventually managed to bribe a guard and made a daring escape.

This former prisoner talked about being kept in isolation and how he longed for someone to sit and just be with him. He also talked about how important it was for him to share his story with a counselor. He shared how Cyanide is one of the most deadly poisons in the world. A single drop on your skin will kill you almost instantly. Imagine if you put a single drop of cyanide in a water bottle. The water would become deadly poisonous. If you took a sip it would likely take your life in an instant. But what would happen if you took that same drop of cyanide and dropped it in an Olympic sized swimming pool full of water? The cyanide would be so dissipated as to become harmless. The same is true of us. When we keep the poison of the grief and heartache we experience inside, it is like that drop of cyanide killing us from the inside. If we share that grief, and talk about it enough, the poison will be dissipated and rendered harmless.

So we might ask the question, "When does God ever weep?"

Another question we may ask is, "Does our suffering even matter to God?" Some people think God is somewhere out there in the ether, and doesn't have time to be interested in us.

We know from scripture that God is acquainted with our grief, and knows our sorrows. Many years ago, there was a shepherd who was made famous by a newspaperman. It seems there was a rumor that this shepherd knew the name of every one of his sheep, and they would respond to him when he called their name.

A local newspaperman thought this story was too good to pass up, so he thought he would go and investigate. If nothing else, it would make an interesting – feel good human interest story. The newspaperman traveled out into the country where the shepherd lived, and found him out among his sheep.

The newspaperman asked the shepherd "Is it true that you know all of your sheep by name, and they know your voice when you call?"

The shepherd said, "Yes that is true. Let me show you."

The shepherd started calling out names, pointing to the various sheep. Every time he would call the name of the sheep he pointed at, they would raise their head and look at him. "Hey Fluffy…Spot… Look here Pete… Spike what are you doing?"

The newspaperman was astonished. He thought there must be some kind of trick. Every sheep looked exactly the same to him. How could he even tell the sheep apart, let alone know each of the sheep by name?

The Shepherd showed him his secret. He said, "You see that sheep over there? He has a brown splotch in his wool. I call him Spot. And over there, that sheep's feet turn in slightly – that's Ducky. That sheep over by the bush, she got caught in some brambles and has a peculiar chink out of her ear… and on and on he went.

It took a few minutes for the newspaperman to realize that every sheep had some flaw that made them different. Even though they appeared at first to be the same, they were not. The shepherd didn't know the sheep by their perfections, but rather he recognized them by their flaws.

Sometimes we think we have to be perfect before God will have anything to do with us. We have to clean ourselves up in order for

God to give us the time of day and we can never be good enough. But the truth is, God loves us just as we are. He sent His son Jesus to die on the cross for us because he loves us – not for how perfect we can be, but in spite of who we are.

God sees our imperfections and says, "You see that one there, his feet kind of point in… See that one, she got caught up with the wrong crowd, and did some things that have scarred her…See that one over there, he has repeatedly given in to temptation and done the wrong thing and later regretted it. I call each of them by name, they know my voice, and I love every one of them."

Jesus says, as the Good Shepherd, "I would not trade for any one of my sheep. They are my children and I love them. In fact I love them so much that I went to Earth and died on an old rugged cross for them."

GOD KNOWS HOW IT FEELS TO LOSE A SON

The fair coming to town used to be such a big deal when I was little. They would bring carnival rides, cotton candy, and games. I used to love to toss dimes to win a drinking glass, or throw darts to pop balloons and win a little trinket. One year, we got to throw ping pong balls, and if we landed one in the colored water of the little fish bowls, we would win a goldfish. My brothers and I all took a turn at this game. In the end, we brought home half a dozen or more gold fish. Unfortunately, most of them died within a few days. But not Spot. Spot was my goldfish. He was gold all over except for one black splotch on his side – thus he earned the name Spot.

Spot lived for several years. He was the only survivor of the carnival fish. I loved my little fish. One day, our school offered to let us bring in a small pet for show and tell. I wanted to bring in my special gold fish, and tell his story. He was a survivor.

I took Spot to school, and he sat on a counter all day. I was so proud of him. Unfortunately, just before school was out, one of the other kids noticed something was wrong with Spot. He was swimming erratically, and looked sick. By the time school let out Spot had died. I was heartbroken.

As a little boy, I wondered if God cared about my little fish. He was such a special pet to me and now he was dead.

Obviously, there are more tragedies in life that are of far more significance than the death of a carnival gold fish, but as a little boy, this was a devastating loss. The emotions I felt were real. In tragic circumstances, when someone very dear passes from this life, people often ask similar questions. "Does God care? Does God understand how I am feeling? The answer is a resounding "Yes".

Some people believe God is far distant. He is too busy to care about his creation, and even if he did, He couldn't possibly keep track of each one of us. If He is not far distant, or pre-occupied, He must be a cruel, heartless tyrant to allow such suffering to take place.

As fathers and mothers, we have little sympathy for those parents who don't care for and protect their own children. In the same way, we would look at a god who created the universe and then left his children to their own devices without a care and with disdain as a cruel uncaring monster. We would consider Him a cruel god.

Fortunately for us, we don't have a Creator that doesn't care for His creation. The Bible makes it clear that He does care for us. The passage in Luke 12:6-7 reassures us, "Are not five sparrows sold for two pennies? And not one of them is forgotten before God. Why, even the hairs of your head are all numbered. Fear not; you are of more value than many sparrows."

It is so comforting to know that the God of the universe is not pre-occupied or too busy for us. He wants us to carry our burdens to Him in prayer. We can lean into Him when our strength is waning, and He promises to always be available to us. God takes it even farther than that. Not only are we His creation, but He calls us His sons and daughters. It says in Galatians 4:6, "And because you are sons, God has sent the Spirit of his Son into our hearts, crying, "Abba! Father!" Instead of Abba, we today would say, "Daddy". So just as an earthly Father cares for their small child, we can go to Him for comfort. 1 Peter 5:7 tells us that we can go to God as our Father, and cast all our anxieties and cares on Him because He cares for us. It says, "Casting all your anxieties on him, because he cares for you."

The greatest proof of God's love for us is that He gave His own son, Jesus Christ to die in our place. We had a debt that we could not possible pay on our own. The only way to pay the debt for our sins was for a sinless person to take on that debt for us. The payment required was death. So does God know how it feels to lose someone dear to Him? Yes! John 3:16 tells us, "For God so loved the world, that he gave his only Son, that whoever believes in him should not perish but have eternal life."

Jesus Christ, as God's only son experienced humanity in its fullness. He knew what it was like to laugh, love, and cry. He knew how it felt to lose a loved one to death. He knew hunger, thirst, loneliness, and feeling hurt, betrayed and depressed. Hebrews 4:15-16 talk about Jesus, our high priest. It says, "For we do not have a high priest who is unable to sympathize with our weaknesses, but one who in every respect has been tempted as we are, yet without sin. Let us then with confidence draw near to the throne of grace, that we may receive mercy and find grace to help in time of need."

Jesus Christ knows and cares about every one of us. He knows about grief in all its colors. Yes we can say conclusively, based on the Bible, God does know about the pain of loss – He knows how it feels, and He cares for us.

In ancient times, when a large ship came near to a harbor that was difficult to enter, the captain would send a lone sailor ahead of the ship in a small boat or dingy. There may be rocks on both sides making it dangerous for the big ship to enter, and there may be a storm raging making it even far more difficult. It took a brave person to go out ahead of the ship. This was often a suicide mission, as the storm, wind and huge waves could easily capsize the little boat. The life of one sailor was sometimes the price of saving all of the other souls aboard the ship.

Once in the harbor, the sailor would drop a heavy anchor with a rope attached that led all the way back to the ship. Then, a little bit at a time, the other sailors would draw the ship carefully and safely into the harbor. This is descriptive of our lives. As we go through life, we encounter many storms at sea. It is at these times we find ourselves looking for safe harbor. The storms in our lives often involve loss, severe challenges, and extreme stress. Hebrews 6:19 and 20 describes it this way: "We have this as a sure and steadfast anchor of the soul, a hope that enters into the inner place behind the curtain, where Jesus has gone as a forerunner on our behalf, having become a high priest forever after the order of Melchizedek." The Lord, Jesus Christ, has gone before us. He drops anchor for us when life is so hard and the grief is so deep that we think we can't go on. Then, when we reach the end of our lives, he has gone before and dropped anchor in the safe harbor of heaven. Day by day we are drawing closer to the time when we shall be with him beyond the reach of the dreadful storms of life on earth. Meanwhile it is up to us to work out our own salvation with fear and trembling.

There is an old seafarers saying for those who have passed away. They would say: *The winds of life continue to fill the sails, which today are anchored in Heavens safe harbor, no longer in peril upon the deep, nor subject to impending storms.*

SECTION III

WHEN OUR SOUL FEELS BROKEN – RECOVERING FROM GRIEF

Chapter 9.

The Crowd Laughs with you all Year - but only Cries for a Day

Every culture is a bit different when it comes to the expression of grief. In the United States we have a melting pot of cultures with a variety of different traditions surrounding how grief is expressed. However crying or any public display of emotion is generally frowned upon. We have little tolerance for emotional outbursts. Even too much celebrating after scoring points in a ball game will earn you and your team a penalty or a foul.

Our society likes to have things neat and clean. Things should be done orderly, follow a step by step agenda, and have a predictable timetable. When things don't fit the mold that society offers, they most often assume that something is wrong. The same is true for a person in grief. Society will allow you a short amount of time to grieve and cry. It is expected after the loss of a loved one but only for a short period of time. They will reject the person who continues on with their mourning for too long.

How many times have you heard a person talk about getting closure after a loss? The conversation usually goes something like this: "It is good that they are having a funeral service in a few days so the family can get closure." Or maybe something like this, "Now that they have made it through the first year without their loved one, they should have closure." We should note that the second year is actually often more difficult emotionally than the first year. We will talk more about the second year grief in the coming pages.

Crying is often seen as a sign of weakness. This is a cultural myth in our country. Crying is actually a reaction to something that triggered emotion or physical pain. It is not an accurate measure of a person's strength or weakness. Some people cry easily and tears can be a sign of joy or pain. Other people were raised to never cry or show emotion, and may have a very hard time shedding even one tear. Crying for some people requires a great deal of strength. It takes courage for these individuals to share their tears. For other people it takes a great deal of strength and courage to hold back their tears and not cry. Some people, especially at an emotional event such as a funeral, will judge people by how much or how little they cry.   It's important to remember that everyone grieves differently. While some people will weep and shed many tears, others may not cry at all.

The expectation of those who grieve in American culture has changed over the years. There was a time when a grieving person was expected to wear black for up to a year. This would quickly identify a person in grief and would allow society to offer the proper response. If a person was wearing all black, you automatically knew they were grieving the loss of a loved one. You would automatically give that person extra grace and understanding. In today's age of fast food and microwaves, society "doesn't have time for such niceties".

The United States as a society has held several different views over the years. If you could somehow take a time machine and go back in time, you would see different views on grief. You would see different ways people grieved if you were able to travel back in time a couple of hundred, or even just a hundred years ago in American society. Our nation used to be a much more religious one than it is today. Most people were Christian, or at least followed the teachings from the Bible. Certainly people were sad after a death, and mourned their loss. However, the hope of Heaven was much more prominent and this faith led people to have an expectation of being reunited with their loved one. Don't underestimate the difference this hope makes. Charles Spurgeon was one of the most prolific and best recorded preachers of the mid 1800s. Here is an excerpt of the sermon he preached at a friend's funeral service called simply, "Mr. Spurgeon at a Funeral". "What does an unconverted man, who does not believe in Christ, think about death? If you were in the catacombs at Rome, you could tell when you were in the Christian part, and when you were in the heathen portion, because, wherever there is a heathen buried, you seem in imagination to hear howls of lamentation, and the inscriptions on the monuments are all full of grief that never can be assuaged, and of complaints against God. But when you come where Christian men are buried, you perceive at once the change of tone; it is, at least, always peaceful, and sometimes it is triumphant. It never can be right for a Christian to weep as though he were without hope, or as though he rebelled against a tyrant instead of yielding to a Father."

Spurgeon made clear the attitude of the majority of society in America. Since they had the hope of Heaven, they also believed they would be reunited with their loved one. And though it was painful to lose their loved one, they would not mourn as hard as someone who had no hope. This attitude was prevalent from the times of the earliest colonists until the Victorian Age which began around the time of Spurgeon. Prior to this period, most scientists were strong Christians, and looked at the Bible as a history book. Sir Isaac Newton, for example, was an English physicist and mathematician who to this day is still considered one of the most influential scientists of all times. It was Newton who formulated the physical science formulas for the laws of motion, and universal gravitation. Newton also taught that the world could not be more than approximately 6,000 years. He came to this conclusion based on the Biblical genealogical records.

In the Victorian age, religion became less prevalent than in previous years. Darwin's Origin of Species, written in 1859, challenged religion. Death was seen more as a failure of modern medicine. Death meant a loss of family, and there was an excessive amount of tears shed, and much more vocal mourning was practiced. Heaven was not assumed any longer by the great majority as it once had been. More people left the faith of their fathers.

After WWI, people began to once again show more restraint in their grief, and shed fewer public tears. This was also a time of revival in America, with more people turning back to God and Christianity. The hope of Heaven was restored to more families. There was a different attitude across the country. Keeping a "stiff upper lip" became the norm and what was expected during this period of history. Men and boys were expected to never cry and taught to suppress their emotions.

Today, we see another shift in what is acceptable bereavement. Men are now encouraged to show their sensitive side. They are expected to cry, but when men do cry most people don't know how to handle it. Women who don't cry are quickly judged as being cold and insensitive. Public tears are OK as long as it looks like we are trying not to cry. Most people don't know what to do when someone is genuinely crying – should they hug them, pat them on the back, or just leave them alone?

In today's society, weeping aloud tends to be something you do at home in private. The exceptions are at a funeral or wedding where tears are expected. But even at these events, excessive crying is frowned upon.

Is there such a thing as too much crying when a person is in grief? Tears can be healing. There is a little ditty that I once heard that may help. "Let em cry until their dry." We shouldn't try to stop a person from crying in most circumstances. Allow them to get the tears out – especially if you are the friend they have trusted to share their grief.

King David often wrote about his grief. He gives a much better example of how we should handle our painful emotions. For example, in Psalm 69:1-2 he wrote, "Save me, O God! For the waters have come up to my neck. I sink in deep mire, where there is no foothold; I have come into deep waters, and the flood sweeps over me." He also talks about the tears that he sheds. Psalm 6:6 says, "I am weary with my moaning; every night I flood my bed with tears; I drench my couch with my weeping." And over in Psalm 56:8 he writes, "You have kept count of my tossings; put my tears in your bottle. Are they not in your book?"

GRIEF AT WORK

Despite society's assumptions about grief and closure, we do not grieve on a timetable. It will take as long as it takes. For some people getting back to normal will come quickly. They may cry on the inside and not shed many tears on the outside. Others will experience heart ache and grief for a very long time.

So how long is long enough? Grief is a journey and it takes time. It can't be rushed. There will probably always be a hole in your heart shaped like the person you have lost. That doesn't mean you can never function again. The person after a reasonable amount of time who finds they cannot go to work, complete regular chores and daily tasks, may need to seek professional help. But just because you have the occasional "memory hug" or shed a few tears when you are reminded of your loved one a year or more after they have passed doesn't mean you are not normal.

Most companies expect us to leave our problems at home and just do what we are paid to do. This is not a realistic request. A person who is having marital problems; extreme financial challenges; or has just lost a loved one will have a very difficult time not thinking about the problems they are having at home. It's almost like telling a person, "For the next five minutes, don't think about pink elephants." The idea is now at the front of your mind and it is nearly impossible to not imagine a pink elephant. In the same way, a business can tell its employees to not think about their personal problems while at work, but it is nearly impossible. It's almost like trying to stop the wind, or hold back the ocean.

Your co-workers may suggest now that the funeral is over; the divorce is finalized; or the loss is past and you have moved on that you should now be over it. The world doesn't want you to ever express sadness or grief with few exceptions. They will say you shouldn't still be grieving because, "You have closure now."

The process of grief is not something that has a clear start and stop point. You can't say, "Here are the five easy steps to grief recovery." The process may have many stops and starts. About the time you think you have finally moved on, you may catch yourself in a memory hug and shedding some tears. It takes as long as it takes.

Most companies typically offer 2 days, to a week off for bereavement leave. If this is something offered to you, take advantage of it but realize you will not be past your grief in such a short period of time.

Chapter 10.

If the Devil can't go, he sends a cynical Christian

We put higher expectations on those who share our faith – other Christians. We expect them to be understanding, supportive, and kind. We never expect them to "kick us when we are down". We never think they will be the ones who will hurt us, or speak harmful things to us. I don't mean to excuse the bad behavior of some, but we often put higher expectations on other Christians than what is fair to ask. We may think, "The world is out to hurt us, but other Christians are our brothers and sisters so we should be able to always trust them to have our backs". For those from big families, we know that sometimes the people who can hurt us the worst are those we are related to - those closest to us.

Christians can hurt us the most because we do in fact often put them on some kind of pedestal. We expect them to be different. After all the bible says in John 13:35, "By this all people will know that you are my disciples, if you have love for one another." We are expected to show love – especially for fellow believers. The problem is Christians are not perfect. We know how we are supposed to act, but we all have struggles trying to be the people God has called us to be.

It may be that the people who say or do things to hurt us have good intentions. The best meaning people can sometimes hurt us by their words or actions. They may not even realize they are being offensive.

Some people are just flat mean. They speak what is on their mind, and expect others to simply take what they have to say. They think they are being direct, or being painfully honest. They excuse their words or actions by saying such things as "I have to tell the truth." Or, "I can't help speaking my mind; or I have always been very direct." These are weak excuses for offending people. The Bible tells us to speak the truth in love, not in spite. These people are simply being insensitive and can be very vindictive.

The Bible warns believers to watch out for "wolves in sheep's clothing". One of the biggest enemies of the sheep is the wolf. The shepherd and the sheepdog are constantly on the lookout for the wolf. If the wolf could disguise itself as a sheep, they could get close enough to kill and injure many sheep before they could be detected. In the same way, there are some who name the name of Christ – who claim to be Christian – who may not be what they appear to be. It is currently in vogue for some atheists to pretend to be Christians, attend church, and by all appearances be followers of Jesus Christ. Their motive is to do damage to true Christians. I have known people who talked like a Christian, acted like a Christian, and went to church regularly. Many people rave about how wonderful they are. But given the opportunity, they use the trust others put in them to destroy those people who trust them. They take advantage of the confidence put in them by Christians to exploit money from them, manipulate them, or misuse them in other ways. Some simply want to cause havoc in the Church. These people may not be Christians at all, but by their example give all Christians a bad name.

For some people – Christians included – their actions are committed on purpose and meant to inflict pain. They may have been hurt themselves, and in some twisted way find comfort in causing others to share their pain. They have become cynical and hard. The world doesn't have a corner on cynical people. Christendom has its share of kooks, and damaged cynical people. The world will be quick to point out so called "Christians" who do damage to the reputation of Christ. Instead of defending their actions, we can tell them, "Yes, we know they are poor examples of what a Christian should be. They drive us crazy too."

On the other hand, some Christians want to be helpful but simply don't know what to say. They may use clichés or quote scripture simply because they feel they have to say something. They want to say the right thing, but it always seems to come out all wrong. There was a time I was sharing how I was going through a very difficult time with a group of Christian friends. It was really hard to talk about. I shared some things from my heart and was about to ask for prayer. One of my "friends" jumped in and told me, "We don't need to pray about this. You simply need to stand in faith.

After all, all things work together for good to them that love the Lord." She quickly dismissed me at that point, and tried to change the subject. Instead of feeling "heard" and lifted up, her words felt like they crushed my spirit. It really hurt. I wished at that point that I hadn't said anything.

There are some things to say when a person is suffering, but a lot more things not to say. Here are few examples of things not to say and how to express them better.

<u>Don't say</u>: "I know just how you feel."
<u>Do say</u>: "I can't begin to know how you feel. All I know is that I love you and hurt for you."

<u>Don't say</u>: "God never gives us more than we can handle."
<u>Do say</u>: "This seems like more than you can stand to bear, and I am here for you."

<u>Don't say</u>: "He/she is happy now because they are with God in Heaven."
<u>Do say</u>: "You made his/her life so happy while they were here on earth."

<u>Don't say</u>: "God took him/her because He needed them more than you."
<u>Do say</u>: "We know you loved them so much, and you must feel a great sense of loss now that they are gone."

<u>Don't say</u>: "God needed another flower for His flower bed in Heaven." Or "God just needed another Angel."
<u>Do say</u>: "Your loved one is important to God and Heaven is a special place."

<u>Don't say</u>: "God allowed this to happen so there must be a reason for this tragedy." Or, "All things work together for good to them that love the Lord…"
<u>Do say</u>: "God is a caring and loving God and He hurts when we do."

<u>Don't say</u>: "It was God's will."
<u>Do say</u>: "I don't know why something this awful has happened to you."

<u>Don't say</u>: "If there is anything I can do, please just give me a call."

<u>Do say</u>: "I see you may need help with _____. If it is ok, I will take care of this for you." Or, "What can I do for you right now?"

There are other clichés, and sayings that are very common. These are things we as a society say when we don't know what else to say. If you stop and think about it, the only person who feels better after saying a cliché is the person who spoke it. Here then are some examples of other terrible things we should never say to someone in grief:

"Don't cry."

"Be brave."

"He/she is at rest now."

"Be glad it's finally over."

"God helps those who help themselves."

"Time heals all wounds."

"God knows best."

"You have to be strong now."

"It's time to get over it."

"Your young, you will find someone else."

"Your young, you can have another baby."

"Where God guides, God provides."

"If God brings you to it, He will lead you through it."

"Be thankful that you have other children."

"All things work together for good."

"You need to just count your many blessings."

"It could have been worse…"

"You need to step up and be the man/woman of the house now."

We know that all scripture is true. There are passages in the Bible that can be very healing and encouraging. Some of our clichés and sayings are actually taken right from the Bible. They may be verses, or truths taken from the pages of scripture. Here are a few examples:

"All things work together for good…" based on Romans 8:28, "And we know that for those who love God all things work together for good, for those who are called according to his purpose."

"God won't give us more than we can handle." Based on Romans 10:13, "No temptation has overtaken you that is not common to man. God is faithful, and he will not let you be tempted beyond your ability, but with the temptation he will also provide the way of escape, that you may be able to endure it."

"Everything happens for a reason…" Based on Ecclesiastes 3:1, "For everything there is a season, and a time for every matter under heaven:"

There are many other clichés based on scripture verses. The thing about many of these clichés and all of the scriptures is they have truth to them. The problem is when they are said in a dismissive way (it is almost impossible for it to not come across this way) they are not helpful to the hearer. There is one more cliché that I think is appropriate to share at this point. The cliché "Better caught than taught" teaches us that some things are better learned on our own rather than having them force fed to us. If a person is grieving, God may lead them to a passage in the scriptures about God never leaving them, or working everything out. This can be very meaningful to that person.

If you don't know what to say at a given moment, you're probably better off not saying anything at all. I often use the example of walking down a grocery store aisle and spotting someone you know who has just had a significant loss. Perhaps their loved one has died. Instead of approaching them, you may be afraid that you don't know what to say and duck down a different aisle hoping they didn't see you.

Most people don't remember what was said to them when they were at their worst moments of grief. What most people do remember is the person who didn't say anything, but just spent time with them and allowed them to grieve. Another useful cliché is "If you can't improve on silence - don't try."

King David often put a pen to paper when he was sad, when he was afraid, or when he was grieving. Reading the Psalms is almost like reading the very private thoughts and personal journaling of this man "after the Lord's own heart". Many of his writings are so personal. Reading the Psalms brings such comfort because in them we can see our own lives. It is as if we are looking at a mirror image of ourselves and what we are going through. They are a good place to turn to when you are grieving.

Most Christians don't mean to be hurtful with their words. In fact, most think they are being helpful by quoting scripture, or spouting clichés. Don't hold it against them. Be patient with them. Sometimes you have to tell them what is or isn't helpful for you right this moment. If they get it wrong, try to understand that they meant well even when it comes out totally off the mark.

Chapter 11.

A Skunk at the Garden Party

No one wants to have to go through grief. Going through grief means something has happened to break our hearts. This most commonly means we have lost a loved one to death. None of us are immune to grief hitting us at some point in our lives.

One of the most difficult times to be going through grief can be during the holidays. Everyone wants us to be upbeat, and happy. They want us to be cheerful and celebrate the holidays. But if we are going through a tough time, we may not want to be smiling and happy. We may want to be quiet, reserved, and somber. We may just want to be left alone for a while.

People tend to avoid individuals who are negative during times of festivity. You may have done the same thing before experiencing grief for yourself. It is a common event. We want to be around people who seem happy and excited all the time. These are the people who are often described as having a magnetic personality that seems to draw people to them.

There are many firsts when we are grieving. The first holidays without a loved one can rock our world view. We see things from a different perspective when we are grieving. The holidays can be depressing even years after a loss. They may bring up memories of spending time with loved ones who are no longer around. Some people make a decision to simply not celebrate the holidays to avoid painful memories. Some people will choose to not even acknowledge the world is celebrating without them. I know people who seem to go into hibernation around Halloween time, and don't come back out until after the New Year.

Some people have a lot of guilt associated with celebrating anything after a loved one has passed away. They seem to think that if they are happy, they are not respecting the memory of their loved one. I can assure you that your loved one who has passed away would never want you to be miserable. They would not want you to withdraw and skip celebrating a holiday because of them.

Sometimes people will overcompensate and try to simply forget all the special memories of their loved one who has died. These people don't want to remember, because they think it will make them sad. They try to stay too busy shopping, and going to parties to be reminded of their loved one. They may turn to heavy drinking during the holidays to numb themselves.

There is another way we can experience the holidays. We don't have to go to extremes. We don't have to be so overwhelmed with grief that we ignore the holidays altogether. We don't have to keep so busy that we don't have time to remember the good times we had with our loved one before they passed. Instead we can incorporate our grief and all of our special memories into our holidays. This may be a really good alternative for those who are grieving and don't know what to do or how to handle the holidays. Here are a few suggestions you may find helpful.

First of all, don't be afraid to grieve. Experiencing grief, especially the first year, is a normal response when dealing with loss. You don't have to walk around with a smile on your face all the time for those around you. They will understand you are missing your loved one, and will give you extra grace. If they don't understand, they are probably not people you would want to be around anyway.

Second, you should cherish your memories. You may not want to talk a lot about your recollections if the death was recent. Your emotions may be too close to the surface and it may be still be too raw to talk about. Sharing your reminiscences can be wonderfully healing. The holidays when friends and family are around can be a perfect time to remember. As the memories begin to flow, don't be surprised if you have a chuckle or two at the funny memories that come to mind.

There are some things you could do to create new traditions and new memories to honor your loved one over the holidays. Maybe it is lighting a special candle in remembrance. Each time you light the candle you can think of them. Maybe you want to serve at a soup kitchen helping out those who are less fortunate. One suggestion that I like is to buy a special ornament in remembrance of your loved one. This ornament may be something that exemplified who they were. If your Dad loved fishing, you might find something to do with fishing. If your mother collected angels, you may want to find a very special angel to hang on the tree. Whatever love or hobby your deceased loved one enjoyed can probably be found recreated as an ornament. Make the special ornament unique so when you place it on your tree every year it will bring a smile and perhaps a tear in remembrance for whom it represents.

Another idea is to use something special of your loved one's during the holidays. This may be such things as your mother's fine china, or a particular decoration they always liked. Maybe there was a particular music cd they really enjoyed listening to, or stuffed animal they would put under the tree. Some people will try to have everyone's favorite dish or dessert at family holiday gatherings. Whatever this special something is it will help you feel a connection with your loved one and bring back warm memories.

If celebrating the holidays this year is too much, it is OK not to celebrate. It may be that your loss was very recent and you just don't even feel like going through all the motions of a holiday celebration. If the tradition is for family to come to your home at the holidays, tell them that you have made other plans and you are not up for it this year. Be sure and let them know you are fine with them celebrating somewhere else this year, and that you will be OK. Make sure you really are OK and that you take care of yourself this year. It is not the "end of the world" if you don't celebrate this year, but don't allow yourself to become so depressed that you do something that your family will regret, such as doing harm to yourself or taking your own life. Suicide can be a realistic concern during this time of year.

Many of you will choose to participate with friends and families in celebrating the holidays this year. Take the time to plan in order to minimize your stress, and maximize the fun. Make the holidays your own. They come around but once a year, and you may be creating memories that will last a lifetime. Christmas is not just pretty lights, wrapping paper and a decorated tree. Contemplate the true meaning of Christmas, and spend some time enjoying the warmth of family and friends as they gather to share life and laughter. Someone once said;

"Christmas is tears and precious memories of times gone by. Christmas is wishes and prayers, sadness and joy.

Christmas is hope."

    Many of you dear readers chose this book because you want to be able to help those who are grieving. I want to take a moment to speak directly to you. Sometimes our best intentions get us into trouble. There are some things that are not helpful to say to a grieving person during the holidays. Let's look at what some well intentioned people have said to the bereaved that were hurtful and should not be repeated:

1. "Don't spoil the holidays for everyone else.

2. "But it's Christmas…" (or Thanksgiving, Easter, etc.)

3. "Your loved one is in a better place so you should be happy about that."

4. "We have to hold our family gathering at your house or it just won't be the same.

5. "Tis the season to be jolly – so get with it."

6. "You just need to stay busy."

7. "What do you mean you aren't decorating your home this year?"

8. "You should be in the holiday mood."

9. "No one wants to be around someone who's always feeling sorry for themselves."

10. "You should be over it by now."

    Some people seem to have the attitude that "It's not the holidays until someone is crying." Of course we know it doesn't have to be that way. We need to have a little patience, and a bit more grace with each other, but especially with those who are grieving. Here are a few things that might be helpful to say or do during the holidays.

1. Share a good memory you have of the deceased loved one, and use their name.

2. Invite them out for coffee, to your home for dinner, etc.

3. Ask them to spend the holiday with your family.

4. Invite them to a special Christmas service at your church.

5. Let them know that you care about them.

A bereaved person will experience a lot of firsts. The holidays will be one of the biggest. However, there are other firsts that need to be considered. When grieving during the first twelve months there may be first birthdays; first anniversaries; first time going to the store alone; first Mother's day or Valentine's day; and many other special occasions. The first anniversary of the death will also eventually come. For many, the second year is more difficult than the first. It's as if the numbness starts wearing off after the first anniversary of the death, and our emotions are more exposed and raw.

It used to be a tradition to wear black when grieving. Most people would wear black for the first twelve months after a loss. This was a clear signal to everyone around to have a little extra grace with the person in mourning. In some ways this was a very helpful tradition.

Some people today will wear their emotion on their sleeves as people once wore black. They can cry, or become very angry at the slightest provocation. They may think "people should know" that they are grieving. This is not fair to those around you. Over time your co-workers, friends, and acquaintances will move on from the loss. The rawness will not last as long for them as it does for the one directly experiencing the loss. It is our turn to have more grace with them. Don't assume they should know what you are thinking or feeling. None of us are very good at mind reading.

The danger in wearing our emotions on our sleeves is that we will drive away the very friends and people who would ordinarily be available to us. Our friends who genuinely care about us would not intentionally be uncaring, or try to hurt us.

There is nothing wrong with expressing grief, or crying. However there are times when it is inappropriate. If you are crying so much that you are not able to function at work, you probably should either not be there, or you need to pull yourself together.

Jesus himself is our best example of "good grief." There are a number of places that mention his weeping. Hebrews 5:7a, "In the days of his flesh, Jesus offered up prayers and supplications, with loud cries and tears, to him who was able to save him from death," He was acquainted with grief and had sorrows just as we do. In John chapter 11 we read the story of how he cried at the death of his dear friend Lazarus. John 11:35 says, "Jesus wept."
Of course we know the rest of the story of Lazarus, how Jesus raised him from the dead.

We know that Jesus wept over his friends, his enemies, and his own death. But we don't ever read that Jesus was so overcome with grief that he "left the ministry", or was no longer able to function. It seems he used his grief to motivate him on to do more good works.

We all need time for grieving when we have a major loss in our lives. It may take us a while to feel like our feet are back under us. But even as Jesus, we need to eventually move on and use the loss that we experience to compel or motivate us to doing good. When Jesus healed Lazarus there must have been a huge celebration in his household. We can't bring someone back from the grave, but we can honor their memory and do something to bring joy and comfort to someone else.

Chapter 12.

Stop the World, I Want Off

There are many life lessons we can learn from nature. It's as if God hid these lessons in plain sight, knowing mankind's natural curiosity would lead us to discover them. There is a little moth that really seems to demonstrate a metaphor for life. The North American Cecropia Moth is a cousin to the silk worm from which we get so many beautiful garments made of silk. This moth gives us a remarkable life lesson. The Cecropia Moth goes through intense struggles throughout its short life. It passes through three stages of development to finally reach maturity as a large beautiful winged moth.

The female Cecropia Moth lays its eggs on a food plant such as a milk weed. When the egg first hatches, the little Cecropia Moth comes out as a caterpillar and immediately starts eating vegetation. It grows rapidly inside of a thick epidermis or skin. The skin doesn't stretch or grow, so eventually it will outgrow its skin. It will be forced to split the old skin and fight its way out of the shell. This is called molting and will occur four times in the life of the larva. Some species will molt as many as ten times.

Eventually the caterpillar will reach its full size. Up until now, it has had the freedom to move around the tree from branch to branch searching for fresh leaves to devour. But now, its next stage involves having to be immobile. The larva will attach itself to a branch and begin spinning a tight cocoon. It will completely encase itself in this silken chamber.

While in its cocoon, the caterpillar will go through an amazing transformation. It will change from a little worm, to a beautiful flying moth. It looks nothing like the ugly little caterpillar it once was.

The Cecropia Moth can produce two to three thousand feet of silk to create their cocoon. The ancient Chinese harvested the silk from the Cecropia Moth as far back as 2600 B.C. They achieved great wealth by harvesting and then weaving the silk into strong but beautiful clothing.

I can remember learning about butterflies and moths as a curious kid in grade school. I was fascinated with how this transformation from a caterpillar to a butterfly or a moth could take place right under my nose in the yard behind my home.

One year we had a tree in our yard that was loaded with caterpillars. I studied them every day after school (this was long before cable TV or video games). I found several caterpillars and put them in a large glass jar along with a big handful of leaves. I wanted to see this transformation for myself.

The jar sat on my dresser for a couple of weeks or so. I regularly put fresh leaves in the jar for the caterpillars to eat. Over time, the larva spun cocoons and hung them from the little branches in the jar. Then one day after school, there were moths in the jar. I was ecstatic!

One by one the moths began unfolding their wings. Their wings came out shriveled and it appeared something was wrong, but soon the wings expanded, hardened, and they flew away.

There was one cocoon that had not fully hatched. There was a hole in the top, but the moth seemed to be struggling to get free, so I carefully took my boy scout pocket knife and cut back some of the silk fibers. This made the hole a little bigger, and the moth was able to crawl free. Without realizing it I had doomed the little moth. The struggle the moth went through was vital to build up its muscle systems. The pressure exerted by the muscles to break free from the cocoon was what would push the blood into the wings causing them to expand. Without this struggle, their wings would not fully expand, they will be crippled, and soon die.

We don't always understand the struggles that we go through. We pray begging God to help us, and relieve the pressure and grief we are feeling. We plead with Him to take away our pain. We don't understand why He doesn't take away our struggles, or why he didn't stop the circumstances that led to our pain in the first place. As difficult as it is to understand – and as hard as it is for us to endure, we would be crippled if we never had to struggle or never went through hardships. The struggles we endure at present are essential to our future life achievements.

There is a wonderful story of tragedy to triumph in the life of King David. The story can be found in the book of I Samuel, chapter 30. This occurred before David became King. He was living in the desert as a nomad in a place called Ziklag. He had drawn quite a following. He was becoming a mighty warrior. A large army of fighting men who believed in his cause had joined him. They were doing battle against the enemies of Israel.

One day, David and his mighty men were returning home from a successful campaign. They arrived at their homes only to discover that their homes had been attacked. Let's look how the Bible describes this scene in I Samuel 30:1-6a: "Now when David and his men came to Ziklag on the third day, the Amalekites had made a raid against the Negeb and against Ziklag. They had overcome Ziklag and burned it with fire and taken captive the women and all who were in it, both small and great. They killed no one, but carried them off and went their way. And when David and his men came to the city, they found it burned with fire, and their wives and sons and daughters taken captive. Then David and the people who were with him raised their voices and wept until they had no more strength to weep. David's two wives also had been taken captive, Ahinoam of Jezreel and Abigail the widow of Nabal of Carmel. And David was greatly distressed, for the people spoke of stoning him, because all the people were bitter in soul, each for his sons and daughters. But David strengthened himself in the Lord his God."

David and his men went from being elated by their recent victory, to being devastated by the loss of everything they had. Their homes were burned, all their belongings were stolen, and their children and wives had been kidnapped. All of them cried bitterly for a long time, weeping until they had no more tears to shed. Their mourning begins to turn to anger. Someone was to blame, and someone needs to pay. David's own men started blaming him, and they wanted to stone him to death.

David had been drifting in his faith, but as is commonly the case, his grief drove him back to God. He began to pray. He sought direct guidance from the Lord on what to do. He asked if he should go after these terrorists who had taken their families. The direction of God was clear. They were to pursue them, and not only would they catch them and face them in battle, they would defeat them and get everything back that they had lost.

David and his men were beaten down and tired. They had just marched 60 miles from the battlefield of their most recent campaign. But despite their weariness, they immediately set out after the raiders double time. The narrative tells us they were so exhausted that 200 of the 600 men who set out after these terrorists collapsed by a brook of water called Besor. Even though their families are in danger, they simply don't have the strength to continue. The remaining 400 men decide to leave much of their gear with the 200 staying behind so they can move faster and expend less energy.

Like an exciting action movie, this small group, against all odds, was pursuing the larger malevolent army. Along the way, they found an Egyptian in the field who appeared to be part of the raiding party they were chasing. He was near death not having eaten or drunk anything in three days. David and his men gave him water and something to eat. Once the man revived, he told them how he had been a servant of one of the terrorists. He had been left to die when he became sick three days earlier. He informed David and his men that indeed this was the same group who had made the raid on their city and had burned everything they couldn't steal or kidnap. 1 Samuel 30:15 picks up what is going on. It says, "And David said to him, "Will you take me down to this band?" And he said, "Swear to me by God that you will not kill me or deliver me into the hands of my master, and I will take you down to this band."

By God's providence, they found this Egyptian man who led them right to the marauding band's camp. They found them having a big party, drinking, eating, and dancing around because they thought they had pulled off this raid against David and his army right under their noses. The Bible tells us that David and his men slaughtered these enemies, and not only got all of their families and belongings back, but all of the livestock and wealth accumulated by this enemy army. The author of 1 Samuel is very specific – nothing was missing. David brought it all back, just as God had told him he would.

It was not easy. The men were exhausted, and their grief had taken its toll on them, but they were able to pursue their enemies, overcome them, and win a huge victory. The victory came after pain and struggle, similar to what we see in nature with the silk bearing Cecropia Moth.

Every stage the Cecropia Moth goes through involves pain and struggle. But every stage is necessary to its growth and maturity. Arguably, the last stage from pupae to butterfly escaping its cocoon prison is the hardest and most painful struggle. But the last stage is also the one that brings the biggest reward and transformation. Just as the moth has to go through the struggle and pain of its transformation, there are no shortcuts to going through grief. We will be the stronger for having gone through our struggles, and better able to help others struggling through grief as well. There are no short cuts through the journey of grief. It is something we have to go through for ourselves. However, there are some things that we have learned that can help and make the journey if not easier, at least not as hard to bear. In the last section of this book we will be looking at coming out the other side of our grief journey and some of the things we need to know to successfully navigate the journey.

Chaplain Terry Morgan

SECTION IV

HEALING FOR OUR SOUL – COMING OUT THE OTHER SIDE OF THE GRIEF JOURNEY

Chapter 13.

A New Path

People may say such things as "I'm glad to see you are back to normal." Or they may say, "You need to get some closure so you can get back to normal."

What is normal? You experience grief because of loss. Unless what has been lost is restored, things will be different from the way they were before the loss. You will reach the point that you have a "new normal" but that will not look the same as what normal looked like before.

Time seems to slow down when grief is fresh and raw. It may feel like you will never get better. It often takes a long time but eventually you will find you are on the other side of your grief. This doesn't mean you will no longer occasionally have memory hugs. It also doesn't mean you will be the same person as you were before your grief experience. You will be different. You will eventually find yourself at a "new normal".

Things in your new normal won't be exactly the same as before your loss. You may have started some new traditions, and new ways of doing things. You may have begun to embrace the faith of your childhood, or explored an area of faith you have never known before.

Most people will not even realize they have transitioned to a new normal. It becomes automatic after a while. Things you once took for granted, will once again become part of your routine, but without what or who you have lost. Those that do realize they have reached that point may feel more confident and self secure, but there may also be a bit of sadness.

King David, the author of many of the Psalms didn't grow up in a royal family. His family was not even considered wealthy, or well off by today's standards. He was the son of a shepherd. Being a shepherd was one of the lowest positions in society. It was a hot, dirty job that most people would not choose for themselves. David's brothers were all shepherds, and in all probability, he would have his own flock of sheep one day when he became mature, got married, and began a family of his own. Of course we know the rest of the story, and how God had other – much bigger plans for David's life.

As a young man David was doing his chores, watching over his father's flock of sheep. King Saul had put out a request for every available man of fighting age to come and assist in the upcoming battle that would inevitably ensue. King Saul had taken his troops into battle against the Philistines – a tribe of terrorists who often made raids on and attacked the Israelites.

David's older brothers had all gone off to do battle answering the king's call for fighting aged men. David's father, Jesse, instructed David to go take a load of cheese and other food items to his brothers, and the commander of the army. Jesse also wanted him to see how his brothers were doing, and how the battle was going. Jesse was concerned for his other sons.

When David arrived where his brothers were, they scolded him for leaving the flock and accused him of just wanting to see the fight to satisfy his curiosity. They called him conceited and wicked. David seemed to ignore his brother's taunts, perhaps because he was so accustomed to them. But he did notice the most gigantic, meanest looking monster of a man he had ever seen in his life! Goliath was a real life giant. He was enormous! He was standing across the other side of a large gulch taunting the Israelites. Goliath gave them the option of sending their best warrior over to fight him. If he won, they would become Israel's servants. But if Goliath won, the Israelite's would submit and become the servants of the Philistines. This was a common practice in those days. Armies would send out their bravest, mightiest warriors to face each other in an individual hand to hand fight to the death. The winner would receive much acclaim. The loser not only would lose his life, but the entire army he served in would become the servants to the opposing army. Goliath was yelling, "I defy the ranks of Israel this day. Give me a man, that we may fight together." (I Samuel 17:10b)

Every time Goliath would appear, and begin bellowing across the divide between the two armies, the Israelites would run away in fear. They would cower in their tents – afraid they would be the ones to be compelled to face the giant. Arguably, King Saul should have been the one to fight Goliath, but he too was afraid.

You probably know the rest of the story. David took up the challenge. A righteous indignation rose up in him against the Philistine giant. How could Goliath or anyone else have such gall as to insult God and the nation of Israel in that way? He went to King Saul and offered to face the belligerent Philistine champion. At first Saul refused to even consider allowing little David to go out. After all, David was a shepherd and Goliath had been a fighting man pretty much his entire life. David explained how he had bare handedly killed both a lion and a bear that had at different times attacked his flock of sheep. David told the king that this Philistine enemy would be no different from the bear or lion. God would give him the strength to defeat this insolent heathen.

King Saul had David regaled in his own armor. He gave him the whole panoply trying to prepare him for the battle. But David took the armor off, and turned down the use of King Saul's weapons. They were unfamiliar and unwieldy for him. Instead he chose to use his sling and a handful of smooth rocks. When dealing with grief battles, many people will try to give you what worked for them. They may insist their way is the only way. As you have probably gathered from this book, there are many good suggestions for how to handle grief but every person is different. What works for one may not work for another. It's important to use the tools that work for you. By the way, David successfully fought with Goliath and won using his own weapon of choice.

Shepherds grow attached to their sheep much the way we grow attached to a beloved dog or cat. They were considered much more than just cattle - almost like part of the family – just like a dog or cat today. Shepherds lived out in nature, and had to protect the sheep from predators. They didn't have modern weapons of the times such as swords and spears, but instead usually carried a staff or long walking stick with a crook at the top. Some, like David, also carried slings. David knew how to face down large predators such as lions, wolves, and bears. When he became king, he was in a busy palace with lots of people vying for his attention. He would often reflect back to the quiet, peaceful days when he was alone in the wilderness with his sheep. It may have been one of those occasions when David wrote one of the most memorable Psalms. Psalm 23 is also known as the Psalm of the Good Shepherd. David understood the relationship of a shepherd with his sheep. The twenty-third Psalm showed the love, care, and protection of the Good Shepherd for His sheep, symbolizing God's love and protection for us. Let's take a look at what David wrote: "The Lord is my shepherd; I shall not want.

He makes me lie down in green pastures. He leads me beside still waters. He restores my soul. He leads me in paths of righteousness for his name's sake.

Even though I walk through the valley of the shadow of death, I will fear no evil, for you are with me; your rod and your staff, they comfort me.

You prepare a table before me in the presence of my enemies; you anoint my head with oil; my cup overflows. Surely goodness and mercy shall follow me all the days of my life, and I shall dwell in the house of the Lord forever."

The Good Shepherd defends his sheep even to the point of death. He leads the sheep to safe areas where they can eat and drink without fear of being attacked. Of course there are times when the shepherd has to seek for lost sheep. One of my favorite pictures of Jesus is one of Him as a shepherd with a lamb being carried around his neck. A shepherd who has a lamb that is prone to wander off will sometimes take the drastic measures of breaking one of its legs with his staff. When he does this, he will carry the lamb around his neck in this way until its leg heals. It seems cruel, but after this experience, the lamb will never leave the side of the shepherd again. A sheep who wanders away from the shepherd is in danger from wild animals, and exposure to the elements.

Psalm 23 talks about how the shepherd leads his sheep through the valley of the shadow of death. Yet the sheep do not fear because they know their shepherd is with them. When I pause to think about this, I reminisce about the times when I have been broken by grief. It may have been from a death, or other types of loss. As painful as those times in my life have been – as dark and dreadful the path – God has been there as the Good Shepherd faithfully watching over me. At times I have been angry with God, and lashed out at Him. But somehow down deep inside I knew He would never leave me or forsake me despite my crying out in anger and fear.

Sometimes we have questions about our suffering from grief. But realizing the reasons for our suffering may be satisfying for our understanding, but a relationship reaches our soul. The relationship we have with God, as our Good Shepherd, can heal us in those times when there seem to be no answers.

A good friend of mine wrote an updated and amplified version of Psalm 23. I thought this was so good that I asked her permission to include it here. So this is Psalm 23 – "A Prayer in the Dark" by Holly Smith-Eaton (used by permission).

"Lord, regardless of how I feel right now, the truth is that you are my thoroughly capable caretaker, my most devoted friend and my infallible guide. You want nothing less than the absolute best for me. You love me more than I love myself and can take better care of me than I can take of myself.

I'm struggling. You're so invisible, it's impossible for me to see you in this darkness, so please help me to sense your presence in a tangible way.

Right now, as an act of my will, I choose to come toward you, to cooperate with you rather than the enemy.

Even though I feel depressed and self-protective, I choose to believe your promises as absolutely legitimate. I choose to push away the awful stuff that feels so real and to exchange it for the actual truth from your viewpoint.

You are the Source of everything I need. I am safe with you. I can be vulnerable when I'm in your care because your love for me is perfect, you will not harm me; and your grace is sufficient for me. You always provide me with good resources. Please help me to reach out and use them.

I choose to lie down and rest at your feet, like a sheep with its shepherd, in the comfort of green pastures that you keep providing for me, even when I am ungrateful or neglect to notice. I choose to walk with you through this valley of shadows and pain, and to intentionally turn my back on evil and thoughts of death. I choose to picture you right here right now, because, in truth, you are actually here with me. It's as if you have prepared a delicious feast for me and are sitting here at the table to eat it with me while the enemy of my soul stalks all around us, eager to destroy me.

Thank you for your protection and companionship. I choose to accept the manner in which you are anointing my head with the holy oil of painful circumstances, using this time to set me apart in order for me to receive the precarious gift of an otherwise unattainable wisdom, for a ministry of empathy which will come with the sunrise. My cup really does overflow as you continuously pour into it blessings I could never have imagined at an earlier time in my life.

Surely, your utter goodness and unfathomable mercy envelop me now and will continue to be with me all the days of my life. Even though, at this juncture, I cannot even begin to imagine what hopeful or pleasant things my future could possibly include, I know for a fact that I will not be alone in it. You've assured me that you'll be with me consistently, no matter what. I know that you won't ever leave me or forsake me because that's what you promised, and you never lie. And because you never lie, you've actually obligated yourself to me to make all this eventually work out for my good because I love you, and you love me, and you've specifically called me and given me a divine purpose.   Therefore, I choose to walk with you throughout my life, one step at a time, so that you can show me the way. And no matter where I go or where I stay, it will be your house I'm living in, with you as my perfect, constant companion forever. Thank you, Lord.

And so be it."

CLEOPATRA'S NEEDLE

In London, England there is a very old beautiful piece of art work called "Cleopatra's Needle." Archeologists believe it came from Heliopolis, Egypt somewhere around 1500 B.C., and it was buried in the sand for about 2000 years. This incredible ancient Egyptian obelisk was carved out of one gigantic piece of rose-red Syene granite weighing about 200 tons.

Cleopatra's Needle was carved with four sides tapering from bottom to top. The tip of the needle is a small pyramid. You may be familiar with the Washington Monument in Washington, D. C. The Washington Monument was made as a copy of Cleopatra's Needle.

The ruler of Egypt gave Cleopatra's Needle as a gift to the people of Great Britain. It was delivered in 1878. The people of Great Britain were thrilled at the arrival of the huge monument. Everyone was very excited. The local schools in London took the day off so the children could witness Cleopatra's Needle being erected. They were witnessing history taking place right before their eyes.

There was an eyewitness account of the event written by Frank W. Borheham, a Baptist minister from England.   He tells the remarkable story of how he and his parents took a long train ride across the country just to watch the placing of Cleopatra's Needle.

Borheham tells of a huge hole dug beneath the obelisk. Space was made in the front of the hole for a time capsule that would be placed in the hole for future generation's centuries in the future to discover. This time capsule was designed to capture a snapshot of life in London at the time. Many items were added including a large number of photographs. They would also include children's toys; a complete set of British coins, copies of the Bible in various languages and a host of other items from the times. They put one more item in the time capsule that was considered the most important article of their day, out of all the objects placed in the time capsule.

Many time capsules have been buried or hidden since the one under Cleopatra's Needle. Each of them have some of the most important items and examples of modern life that can be obtained. What do you suppose would be considered important enough to be included If we were putting items in a time capsule today on American soil? What do you imagine would be the most vital piece of information that could be passed to future generations? Would the message be a mathematical equation from Albert Einstein – $E=mc2$? Or maybe the most important thing would be the political philosophy of our time that has become so prevalent in our society of being "Politically Correct." Perhaps it would be the electronic schematics for a modern cell phone – since they have become such a common part of today's society.

The organizers of the time capsule to be placed under Cleopatra's Needle said they wanted it to be opened in the 50th century. The obelisk was carved 3500 years before, when Egypt was the greatest nation on Earth. They wanted the time capsule to be opened in approximately the same amount of time from Ancient Egypt to England in 1874.

The message that was placed in the time capsule was considered so important that it was translated into every known language on earth. What was that message? The message was written in two hundred thirty different languages. Here is the message that the leadership of Great Britain thought was so important to share with a generation 3500 years in the future. "For God so loved the world, that he gave his only begotten Son, that whosoever believeth in him should not perish, but have everlasting life" (John 3:16). This was considered the most important message known in the 20th century England.

Many people today would be surprised and astonished by this fact. The message of the Gospel of Jesus Christ was considered more important than any other mystery that could be revealed to the 50th century. The good news of John 3:16 is a mystery that was hidden from the foundation of the world – much longer than the planned time for the time capsule under the monolithic obelisk on the bank of the Thames River in London, where it still stands today. The mystery is that God would send His own son to die for our sins. Jesus Christ loved us so much that he chose to die rather than ever live without us.

Perhaps you are one who is not familiar with the story of the Gospel of Jesus Christ. Here is a brief summary. The Bible tells us that God created the earth, and the entire universe. He made man and woman in His image, and had perfect fellowship with them (see Genesis 1-3). God gave them specific instruction on their purpose aside from enjoying being in the presence of God. They were to care for and tend the Garden of Eden, where they were placed, and could eat anything from the garden. However, there was one tree that they were not to eat from. If they ate fruit from that tree they would cause sin to enter the world, and through that sin death. God wanted to know that Adam and Eve would obey Him out of love, and not because they felt compelled to obey. With so many good things to choose from, surely they wouldn't rebel and eat from the one and only tree in the entire beautiful garden they were told not to eat from. It sounds just like humanity today. We always want the one thing we can't have. We choose things that are bad for us because we don't want to be denied what we want.

Eventually, Adam and Eve were tempted and gave in to the temptation to eat the forbidden fruit. They committed sin and introduced sin into the human race. God is a holy God, and we are told that He cannot tolerate even being in the presence of sin. Adam and Eve were forced out of the Garden of Eden. They were given animal skins from animals in the garden to cover themselves with. This established early on that sin required shed blood as payment. Adam and Eve went on to have many sons and daughters. God had commanded them earlier to fill the earth. The Bible tells us they had many sons and daughters. But every one of their children were born with a stain on their soul that they could not wash away. Every one of them inherited the sin nature of their parents. As they began to marry and have children of their own, this sin nature was passed to every one of their offspring. This has continued down through history to every generation till today. Jesus Christ was the only person ever born sinless – born of a virgin.

Throughout the Old Testament you can read the history of salvation. It tells us of a system of animal sacrifice that was set up to cover the sins of the people. Unfortunately, the blood of the slain animals could not get rid of sin. It could only cover it. It would take a perfect sacrifice, by one who had never sinned – Jesus Christ – to die for once and for all to wash away our sins.

The punishment for sin is death. Nothing else will do. Every one of us deserves to die for our sins. Jesus Christ came to earth to die in our place. He took the punishment of our sins upon himself when He died on the cross in our place.

Some people will say they have never committed a sin. However, Romans 3:23 tells us, "for all have sinned and fall short of the glory of God," This tells us that everyone has sinned without exception. If you observe an infant you will quickly see that a child doesn't have to be taught how to rebel. It comes naturally to them. They have to be taught to be kind, to share, and to behave. If you have ever told a lie, even once, the Bible says you have sinned. If you have committed a sin, even once, you are a sinner.

Some will say that there are many ways to Heaven, and that we should not be judgmental of other religions. The problem with that idea is that Jesus Christ himself said in John 14:6, "Jesus said to him, "I am the way, and the truth, and the life. No one comes to the Father except through me." Jesus Christ was clearly saying there is only one way to get to Heaven. If there was another way for people to get to Heaven, then why would Jesus have to die on the cross? The Bible makes it clear that Jesus did have to die, and without this perfect sacrifice, and shedding the blood of a sinless person, there is no remission, or cleansing from sin. Without his death on the cross there is no forgiveness.

So if we have all sinned, we all need forgiveness of our sins. In John 3:16, Jesus tells us, "For God so loved the world, that he gave his only Son, that whoever believes in him should not perish but have eternal life."

The Bible is very clear on the fact that the perfect sacrifice for sin was Jesus Christ. He died for you, and for me. He not only died, but three days later he rose from the dead, proving He had conquered sin and death. Romans 10:9 tells us what we must do to receive the free gift of forgiveness of our sins. It says, "because, if you confess with your mouth that Jesus is Lord and believe in your heart that God raised him from the dead, you will be saved."

Some people say they have done things too horrible to ever be forgiven. They say such things as, "You have no idea the things I have done. There is no way God would ever forgive me." But the Bible says in 1 John 1:9, "If we confess our sins, he is faithful and just to forgive us our sins and to cleanse us from all unrighteousness." I remember a story from a few years ago of some communist soldiers who were defecting. They risked everything, and left all of their belongings behind to escape their country. To be caught would mean torture and imprisonment, followed by humiliation and a public execution. When they were asked why they were risking so much to defect, they said it was because of the forgiveness found only in Jesus Christ. No other religion offers forgiveness for sins. Each soldier told how they found the horrible, despicable things they were forced to do as soldiers filled them with overwhelming guilt and self condemnation. The forgiveness for their atrocities and sins could only be found in Jesus Christ and the free salvation He offered. Only Jesus Christ offered forgiveness. These communist soldiers found forgiveness and an inner peace that was worth any price. They would give up everything they had, and everything they were for this opportunity to serve the one who forgave them.

The gift of salvation, the forgiveness of our sins, is a free gift. It is not something you can earn by being good enough. As a matter of fact there is nothing you can do to earn it. All you can do is receive it. No matter what you have done, God can offer you forgiveness and a new life. If you would like to accept this free gift of salvation, you can pray a simple prayer. Prayer is just talking to God. You can pray something such as this: *"Dear Heavenly Father, I know I am a sinner, and there is nothing I can do to change that on my own. I believe that Jesus Christ died on the cross for me, for my sins, and rose again three days later for me. Please forgive me of all of my sins, and become my savior. I accept your free gift of salvation. Thank you Father God. In Jesus name I pray these things, amen."*

If you prayed this prayer, and you meant it, you are now a Christian. It is important that you get involved in a Bible believing Christian church where you can learn more and grow in your new life. You need the support of other believers – and they will help you learn and grow in your new found faith. Read your Bible, and spend time in prayer on a regular basis. This will not only help with your new Christian walk, you will find that it will help you work through your grief and receive the support from God that you are looking for.

Chaplain Terry Morgan

Chapter 14.

Practical Suggestions

Our minds are remarkable. God created us in such a way that we can remember things that happened to us as a small child. Yet we can forget what we had for breakfast this morning. Our grief may cause us to dwell on the details surrounding the death of our loved one. The nearer we are to the passing the harder it is to remember the good times we had together. We may have to work at it to remember the memories we made in life especially when the grief is new. It is healing for us to remember what made us smile and laugh – those days of life rather than settling in on the death.

Often times during the wake or the reception following a funeral service people will sit around and start bringing up stories from the past. As the stories begin flowing more and more freely, it is not unusual for humorous memories to come out. You would think this should be a time for somber sadness, but we tend to go to the stories and memories that bring a smile to our faces, or even cause us to break out into laughter. Before you know it, everyone is laughing and sharing funny memories.

Some people will get the strange notion that they will never laugh again after a tragic loss. It's OK to laugh.

It's important for us to get plenty of rest, a little exercise, and eat a balanced diet. Good self-care is no more important than when you are doing the work of grieving. Be sure to drink plenty of water, and avoid excessive alcohol. As you hydrate your physical body, it will be better able to deal with the emotional stress put on it.

When grief is very new and fresh, it can cause us to be easily distracted. Be careful when driving an automobile. Our cars are often a place of refuge from the world, and can be a very personal private place for us. The refuge of our car seems to just invite memories and sad thoughts that can cause our mind to wander. Instead of paying attention to the road, we can easily become so distracted as to be a danger to ourselves and others. If you have to drive purposely avoid thinking about your grief until after you reach your destination. If your mind starts to wander, use your self-talk – that little voice in your head to tell yourself you cannot think about this right now.

Surround yourself with safe people. These are those friends and loved ones who are not likely to say hurtful or inconsiderate things. This is not a time to be "politically correct" and spend time with everyone, even if they bring you down. You probably have a pretty good idea of those who will be helpful and healing for you to be around right now. This may mean not spending time with that long time friend who tends to "speak their mind" or who you find amusingly cynical.

If your grief is from losing a loved one, consider writing them a letter. Tell them what you will miss about them, and what they will miss since they are no longer here. This is a letter you never have to mail. You never have to share this with anyone else, so tell the person who passed how you really feel. Be honest and if you are feeling angry at the person who died, or hurt because they left you tell them that. Sometimes just being able to express what you are thinking and feeling can be very healing.

Be easy and gentle with yourself. Remember your spirit has been wounded. Something very valuable and dear to you has been taken away and you are experiencing the loss. Don't be too hard on yourself. This would be a good time to pamper yourself a little more than normal.

Grief has often been described as a roller coaster ride with lots of ups and downs. You will probably experience a lot of different emotions. Over time, you will likely have good days and bad days.

It may be weeks, months, or a year later before the numbness really goes away. As time goes by and the shock of the loss begins to wear off, you may find yourself feeling worse instead of better for a while. You may start thinking you are as crazy as you can be without being locked up. However, this is a normal experience that many people go through. Given a little more time, the good days will outnumber the bad days. You may want to keep a personal journal or diary about how you are feeling from day to day. You will be able to start seeing a pattern as you look back over your journal.

Take the time to embrace your faith. Most churches recognize that grieving people need special help, and offer services and ministries to assist them. Even if you have not been to church in a long while, they will be ready to embrace you.

Some people believe that God is too busy for them, and even if He is not too busy he is not interested in them. I once heard a thought provoking parable about a man who was distant from God. This man believed that God was too busy for him. He dared God to speak specifically to him. He prayed something like this: "God, you spoke to Moses out of a burning bush. Here is a bush, so if you are there, light this bush up with fire and speak to me and I will believe in you. God, you brought down the walls of Jericho for Joshua. Here is an old wall. If you knock this down, I will know you heard me and I will become a Christian. God you walked on the waters of the Sea of Galilee, and you stilled the storm for the disciples. Here is an ocean, just still the wind and waves and I will follow you from now on." The man plopped himself down by a bush, near an old wall, overlooking the ocean.

God did in fact hear the prayer of this man. He did send fire and speak, but he sent the fire of the Holy Spirit to revive a church. He brought down a wall, but not one made of brick, but the wall of sin that separates man from God. God also stilled the wind and waves. But he didn't still the waves beating on the shore, but the storm and the waves beating on a soul crying out to God.

God waited for the man to respond. He waited, and waited, and waited. But the man was looking at bushes not hearts: he was looking at bricks and mortar, not lives: and he was looking at the sea instead of at souls. The man decided that God had not done anything. He looked up to Heaven and said, "God, have you lost your power?" And God looked down at him and spoke to his heart saying, "My son, have you lost your hearing?"

Remember it is healthy to shed a few tears. If you feel like crying, let the tears flow. Over time the tears will come less and less frequently. Sometimes the best night's sleep will come after the release from a good cry. But don't feel bad when you no longer feel like crying anymore. It's OK to feel good again.

Listening to soft, soothing music; reading a good book; or watching a funny movie can often lift one's spirits. Many people find solace in reading the book of Psalms. King David had such a way with words not only in describing what caused him grief, and how it made him feel, but how he was able to get relief by turning to God.

The Psalms bring comfort as we are able to finally have the right words for what we are feeling.

Fanny Crosby was an incredible song writer from the nineteenth century. She wrote over 6,000 hymns – many of which are still sung every Sunday in churches across our nation. Miss Crosby suffered a great deal physically. She was blind and often felt alone and vulnerable. She found much of her comfort in the Psalms. An example is Psalm 27:4-5 which reads,
"One thing have I asked of the Lord, that will I seek after: that I may dwell in the house of the Lord all the days of my life, to gaze upon the beauty of the Lord and to inquire in his temple.

For he will hide me in his shelter in the day of trouble; he will conceal me under the cover of his tent; he will lift me high upon a rock."

From this Psalm she wrote the beloved hymn, "He Hideth my Soul." Read the beautiful lyrics as you think of this blind woman as she leaned in to her savior.

1. *A wonderful Savior is Jesus my Lord,*
A wonderful Savior to me;
He hideth my soul in the cleft of the rock,
Where rivers of pleasure I see.

- *Refrain*
  He hideth my soul in the cleft of the rock,
  That shadows a dry, thirsty land;
  He hideth my life in the depths of His love,
  And covers me there with His hand,
  And covers me there with His hand.

2. *A wonderful Savior is Jesus my Lord,*
He taketh my burden away,
He holdeth me up and I shall not be moved,
He giveth me strength as my day.

3. *With numberless blessings each moment He crowns,*
And filled with His fullness divine,
I sing in my rapture, oh, glory to God!
For such a Redeemer as mine.

4. *When clothed with His brightness transported I rise*
To meet Him in clouds of the sky,

*His perfect salvation, His wonderful love,
I'll shout with the millions on high.*

Through the years the Psalms have been inspiration for countless songs and hymns. They have often provided solace and comfort to those who are suffering pain.

There are many self help books, and books on grieving. Many of these are in the form of devotionals – with a short reading for every day. These devotionals can give us insight and hope for each day. There is a list of a few other devotionals and other such resources at the end of this book.

Many support groups exist to help those who are grieving. There are many groups designed for specific kinds of grief. These support groups are made up of people who have been on the same journey you currently are on. Some of their members are just starting this journey, some have been grieving for a while, and some have survived their grief and come out the other side. Support groups can offer strength, wisdom, and advice to those at all stages of the grief journey.

Eventually, the day will come when you will consistently feel better. You will feel like you have finally gotten off the emotional roller coaster. You will have recovered from your grief, and you will go on living. This is what your loved one would have wanted for you. For some people the process never really comes to an end, but it gets easier to deal with over time. Remember, It's OK to move on.

Chapter 15.

Memory Hugs

Grief can bring memories into sharper focus. It can be a prompt for tears and emotion that take us by surprise. The trigger can be something as simple as a scent from a familiar perfume – a memorable sight – or an unseen but felt presence. These can be labeled as "memory hugs."

Long after my parents passed from this life I would have brief thoughts of dropping by to visit them. Sometimes I would think about stopping by to ask their advice on some decision I was trying to make. Then it would hit me that they are gone. This thought would be accompanied by a gentle tugging on my heart strings reminding me of my loss. Often a single tear would drop from my eye.

There was once a woman who stopped by a chaplain booth we had set up at an event we were helping with. Let's call this woman Jane. Jane came specifically to speak to a chaplain. She said she had been married for eighteen years before divorcing. Jane said her husband was intolerable and incredibly difficult to live with. A couple of years after their divorce, her ex-husband passed away suddenly. This occurred over twenty years ago. Jane worked an extremely busy job after divorcing, which was both fulfilling and challenging. She was laid off from her job, and decided to take an early retirement. Now, with a lot more free time on her hands, Jane shared that she now finds herself remembering her ex-husband and crying. She asked, "Where are these emotions coming from? I thought they were gone a long time ago." I explained to Jane that what she was experiencing – given the circumstances - was normal. She was having some memory hugs. I gave her some other suggestions to help her move on through her grief journey, and prayed with her. I ran into Jane at another event a few weeks later. She told me she was doing much better and was thankful for the assistance.

There was an elderly mother who lost an adult daughter in a fatal car crash. She shared with me that she knew the exact time of the crash as her daughter's watch was smashed in the crash that took her life. The coroner said she had been killed instantly. Her daughter had died at 12:34 a.m. This elderly mother had been notified of the death about an hour later. The fateful knock on the door by a chaplain with a police officer in the wee hours of the night told her the news no parent ever wants to hear – her daughter was dead and would not be coming to see her again.

This elderly mother told me how starting the very next night, a loud knocking at her door would awaken her at exactly 12:34 a.m. This went on for several years. Every night at the same time, she would be awakened from her sleep. For a while she would go to the door expecting someone to be there, and find no one there. She thought her daughter may be haunting her or something.

One day this elderly mother told me her story. It had been four years since her daughter's tragic death. Each night since then, she would get the haunting knock at her door. As she shared her story, she began to weep. I told her that perhaps what she was experiencing was a memory hug. The knocking that came every night at the same time her daughter had been killed years before was some kind of message. Maybe it was her daughter, not trying to haunt her, but trying to tell her that she was OK and in Heaven and that she shouldn't worry. Perhaps she was saying she loved her as she didn't get a chance to say goodbye. I told this dear senior mother, the next time she heard that knocking in the middle of the night, just say, "I know your o.k. daughter, and I love you too."

I didn't see the grey haired mother for several weeks. I finally bumped into her again at a function and she quickly made her way over to me. She said, "Chaplain – I did what you said. The knocking came at my door at 12:34 in the morning and woke me up. I said "I know daughter and I love you too." She said, "You know what Chaplain? That was the last time I have heard that knocking." I ran into this gentle soul from time to time over the course of several years and every time she would see me she would smile and say there had been no more knocking at her door after midnight.

Perhaps you have lost a loved one and you happen to drive by a favorite hangout or smell their cologne. Some powerful reminder of your loved one brings an unexpected tear to your eyes. I like to call these surprising moments a "memory hug". We don't see them coming, and even if we did we probably wouldn't stop them if we could. They remind us of someone who was very special to us.

Memory hugs are common after the loss of a loved one. They can also come after any kind of loss. It may be you hear about something that happens where you used to work before being let go. A song may come on the radio that was a favorite of you and your ex-spouse. Or maybe a favorite pet died, and you see his favorite toy laying in the yard. Memory hugs are not exclusive to the loss of a loved one, but they can surprise us all the same.

The Bible talks about the grief David felt when he learned of the death of his best friend, Jonathan. You may recall that Jonathan was the son of King Saul – the same King Saul who was sworn to kill David. But David and Jonathan were the closest of friends. The Bible describes their friendship as being closer than brothers.

Despite David slaying the giant Goliath, and saving the Nation of Israel, Saul hated him. It may partially be because of David's popularity among the people. Whatever the reason, Saul tried to get Jonathan to conspire with him to kill David. Because of their close friendship, Jonathan told David he would do anything in his power to help him. In fact, he warned David on several occasions of Saul's intentions to kill him. Jonathan loved David with a friendship that meant more to him than his own life. When David heard that Jonathan had been killed, it nearly broke his heart. He broke down and cried, and refused to eat for a while.

David was a skillful musician and poet. That was one of the reasons Saul asked David to live in the palace with them in the first place. His playing on the harp was the only thing that seemed to bring peace to him. The Bible describes how Saul was tormented by an evil spirit, and the music played by David would calm him. David decided to write a poem about Saul and his son Jonathan. He put the poem to music. He called it "The Song of the Bow" and ordered that all of the people of Judah learn the song. We don't know for sure, but perhaps this song was sung at the anniversary of Jonathan's death.

David wrote the song about Jonathan as a way to help him work through his grief. He expressed his grief over the loss, and the anger at the enemy for killing his friend. He wishes their fields would not produce any crops, and that life in general would be bad for them.

David went on in his song expressing his sorrow by talking about how well respected and loved King Saul and Prince Jonathan were. He talks about their prowess in battle and how the people admired them. He says in II Samuel 1:25, ""How the mighty have fallen in the midst of the battle!"

The song is concluded with David expressing his great love for his best friend in the world Jonathan. I have to imagine that he had many memory hugs as he was reminded of his friend.

Later, perhaps after a memory hug, David found out that Jonathan had a son. His son's name was Mephibosheth. King David gave him and his family such a royal treatment in honor of Jonathan. He told Mephibosheth that he was always welcome at his table to eat with him. He gave all the land that belonged to his grandfather, Saul, to him. This took Mephibosheth out of poverty, and made him a very wealthy man.

Matthew 5:4 tells us, "Blessed are those who mourn, for they shall be comforted." Mourning is God's way of bringing healing to the grieving heart. He uses these memory hugs to gently soothe away the pain. God used David's grief as an opportunity to heal old wounds. Mephibosheth feared for his life because of the way his grandfather acted towards David. Instead he got grace, land and a seat at the king's table.

Many things can cause us to stop and reminisce about deceased loved one. Holidays and anniversaries in particular can be triggers for us. They can come with a lot of memory hugs and set off unexpected emotions. These are normal and will not come as often as time goes by. We still may be surprised when a memory is triggered by the slightest thing, but it is a normal part of the grief journey. Sometimes a memory hug can be a catalyst for us to do something. We may need to let someone or something go – or we may need to take action to mend some relationship.

Chapter 16.

Helping others through their grief journey

Having come so far through our loss and grief, we have gained something. There comes a special calmness and depth to our soul that we never knew before. This calmness is not something we wish for anyone because it is born of terrible hurt and pain. We are able to smile again now – perhaps not as bright and innocent as it once was – but smile all the same. In losing the innocence we once had we have gained a compassion and gentle strength that would never have been gained any other way. We now have a unique perspective on grief that we are able to use to help others.

When a person has experienced the kind of grief that hurts so bad it seems to kidnap our souls, we can minister in a more compassionate way to those who are grieving. When those who have been broken and healed speak to a broken heart it is like giving nourishment to a starving child. There is a depth to our words that seems to pour a healing balm into their wounds. We are an example of survival to those who are just starting their grief journey. Just by being present, we testify that it is possible to endure.

We who have felt the sting of grief, who have experienced the pain of loss, are often the best at helping others. It's important to have a good understanding of the stages of grief. Knowing these stages will help you in ministering to those who are in the midst of their grief. 2 Corinthians 1:3-4 describes this saying, "Blessed be the God and Father of our Lord Jesus Christ, the Father of mercies and God of all comfort, who comforts us in all our affliction, so that we may be able to comfort those who are in any affliction, with the comfort with which we ourselves are comforted by God."

We can relate to the pain others are feeling, because we have experienced pain too. It may not be exactly like our grief journey, but the pain is similar. The next few pages will give you some tools to help others work through their grief starting with the stages of grief that people will experience.

The grief reaction can be broken down into three basic divisions or stages. These stages are the impact stage, recoil, and the recovery stage. Here is a look at each division, with an explanation of their meaning.

THE IMPACT STAGE:

The impact stage is the initial reaction to a loss. This may be brought on in a variety of ways. You may receive a knock on your door and receive the tragic news of the unexpected death of a loved one from a chaplain. Perhaps you are at the hospital when a doctor tells you they did everything they could to no avail. Whatever the method of delivery, the message is life changing. This news has often been described as feeling like you were just kicked in the stomach. It can take your breath away. Some people get a feeling of being light headed, and it is not uncommon for a person to actually faint.

There are a number of mental or emotional reactions that occur during the impact stage.

1. **Trouble Coping:** Some people say they have a hard time managing. They talk about a feeling like they are unable to come to grips with what has happened. It is simply too much to deal with. Our mind cannot wrap itself around the fact that a loved one has died. It's too much for us to process.

2. **Denial:** There is often a period where a person refuses, or simply cannot believe their loved one is gone. This is a natural defense mechanism. There is too much information for our minds to deal with at one time. It is normal for us to experience a period of denial when our mind receives information that is too terrible to accept.

3. **Fear:** Fear is also a common reaction during the impact stage. We may be afraid of what has happened, and what

will happen next. A child has a need to feel safe, and the person who made them feel safe may be gone now. Children may be afraid because they don't feel secure any longer.

4. **Maximum Stress:** The impact stage is a period of absolutely maximum stress. Most people will feel like they can't possible take anything more. It can feel overwhelming.

Our physical bodies will react to the impact of bad news. Our bodies will fight with all of the defenses they have to protect us from bad news, and try to soften the blow. Studies have shown that our bodies react to an emotional threat the same way it does to a physical threat. Our bodies will dump thousands of chemicals into our system. These chemical dumps are designed to help us survive a physical attack – to fight back or run away. Here are a few of the physical reactions that are common during the impact stage:

1. **Heightened senses:** God designed our bodies to survive. You have probably heard of the concept of "Fight or Flight". This idea is that we are equipped to survive by either fighting or running away. One of the ways our bodies will fight for survival is by dumping adrenaline into our bloodstream. The adrenaline can then heighten our senses to hyper states. In other words we will be able to see, or hear extremely well. Chaplains are trained to understand this phenomenon, and will talk softly to people in the impact stage. Some people have described a whisper as someone yelling at them during the impact stage. Others have described time as seeming like it was at a standstill as if everything is moving in slow motion.

2. **Physical Symptoms:** Some people will experience loose bowels, or stomach upset. You may have sweaty palms, and your heart may start beating a lot faster. Some will be light headed, or have bad head-aches. Tightness in the shoulders and chest

area is also common. Though not as common, some people will have shortness of breath, and when combined with other symptoms they may think they are having a heart attack. Please note, if you have symptoms of a heart attack, you should always seek immediate medical attention. Don't ignore these symptoms.

The impact stage generally lasts from a few minutes, to a few hours, and sometimes a few days. Some of the symptoms may even last a few weeks or more.

II RECOIL

After the impact stage, comes the recoil stage. A person will usually physically, emotionally and mentally reach the recoil stage in a few minutes to an hour after the initial impact of receiving bad news. The mind will have had enough time to process what has happened. A trained chaplain will be listening for verbal cues that a person has moved from the impact to the recoil stage. A person in the impact stage will speak of a loved one who has died in a present tense, e.g. "John loves fried chicken." "Sally is a great piano player." "Billy has a good sense of humor." Etc. When a person moves from impact to recoil, their verbal cues will change. They will say things a little differently, such as "John loved fried chicken." "Sally was a great piano player." And "Billy had a good sense of humor." Etc.

A person cannot begin to recover from grief until they are in a past tense process, i.e. they need to move from denial to acceptance. When a person is in denial, they will continue to speak about their loved one as if they are still alive. A person can get stuck in denial if not gently encouraged to accept the loss of their loved one.

There is a method that has proven very effective in helping a person move through denial to acceptance. Shift your speech from a present tense (he is) to a past tense (he was). This will gently encourage the person to shift their thinking. If you pay attention, you will likely witness this shift. Listen for them to change their speech from present tense to past tense as you speak to them.

They will subconsciously shift their speech to past tense. This is an outward sign that they have begun to mentally accept the death.

The recoil stage also has specific emotional responses. Where the impact stage often has a lot of denial, and sadness, the recoil stage is usually marked by anger, protest, bitterness and guilt feelings. During this stage, a person will often start talking about the "If onlys". They may say such things as, "If only I would have been home early, this would not have happened." Or, "If I could do things all over again, it would end differently." Or, "I wish I would have done _____."

Loneliness really begins to set in during the recoil stage. During this stage grief will become more pronounced and mourning will take place. Especially early on it will be very difficult to not express grief. There may be a lot of tears, and they may come at unexpected times. It will take time for our emotions to not surface at the slightest encouragement.

Those in the recoil stage may express "How can I go on?"

We need to help them find or get a need to go on. They may need to go on for their pet cat, after all who would take care of it? Everyone has a reason to survive but they may need assistance to help them find that reason.

They may express a yearning for the deceased not to be dead. They may start looking for the deceased. They may say something like, "He isn't really dead; he will be home in just a few minutes".

They will show a desire to be with others, relatives, friends, neighbors, etc.

When a person receives very bad news, they may experience symptoms of shock. They will be very vulnerable to their environment, and what is going on around them. How we react is how the survivor will tend to react. If we become loud and emotional, they will also. If we are quiet, and talk softly, they will also begin to calm down and talk softly and quietly.

III RECOVERY

The recovery stage may start within a few minutes to a few hours. Everyone grieves differently, so it is hard to put a timetable on the recovery stage. The recovery stage will last for a longer period of time than the other two stages, and may be visible even years later. Many studies show even five years later that people are still in the recovery stage.

There are some things that will often mark when a person begins entering the recovery stage. People will realize they will go on, but will also realize that things will be much different from before.

People who have lost a loved one understand they may have to develop a new set of functioning roles. They may have to set up a new social life. If they lost a husband or wife, there may be sets of mutual friends that are now uncomfortable to be around. They may have originally started out as friends of the now missing spouse, and the relationship may be totally different without him or her. There may even be jealousy on the part of the husband or wife of the friend and a fear that the surviving person may begin pursuing an affair with their spouse.

If the deceased loved one was a child, the child's friends who may have been regular visitors may stop coming around. Everything is different now. It's important during the recovery stage to maintain a healthy support system – but these may or may not be former friends.

Just because a person has begun the recovery process it doesn't mean they will not experience emotional upheaval. The recovery process is a long term commitment. They may still feel anxiety, fatigue, and a lot of stress for quite a while – weeks or even months later.

Life will start interrupting our thoughts as we move through recovery. Those who are grieving will no longer be constantly dwelling on their loved one who has passed. Eventually there will be no more evidence of denial.

Given time, people will usually recover from deep grief on their own - even when left alone. However, it has been shown that people recover much more quickly, and with less lingering issues after the intervention of a caring person. This is especially true when the person doing the intervening is a well trained Chaplain.

PRACTICAL SUGGESTIONS

There are a few practical things we can suggest to others who are just starting out on their grief journey. Some things will help give us hope, bring balance back to our lives, and change our perspective. Many people find that they get their balance back by spending time in nature. This can look like nature walks, sitting by a stream, or going to the ocean. Some people who live in big cities can go spend time in a park. Something about being in nature just seems to bring us back into balance, and helps us by restoring our natural rhythm. Here are a few other suggestions that may help.

1. We can encourage them to embrace their faith while they are grieving. God can be a comforter to our souls and give us strength to endure.

2. They should not try to go through this journey alone. There are a lot of pitfalls along the way, and it is easier if we have a traveling companion who can help us back to our feet. Help them to identify someone in their church or place of worship that is in charge and let them know they are grieving a loss.

3. Encourage them to let their church step in and help. Early on a church body may help with meals for a few days. Later, it may be grief counseling, support, and advice on how to handle day to day things. They may not have been responsible in the past to do certain chores. Now they have to take care of car repairs, taxes, running the lawn mower, etc.

4. They should attend services at the church of their choice. It may be they have not attended services in some time. Perhaps now is the time to return to church.

5. Support groups can make a huge difference in the life of someone who is grieving. The church may have a grief care or other group that meets regularly they can become involved with.

6. There may be opportunity to do something special in memory of their loved one. This may be a special service specifically for them, or a special gift given to a charity in their memory. Some people will plant a tree, or set up a memorial bench, or plaque.

7. If a tree or bench is outside of their budget, perhaps they could give a bouquet of flowers.

8. Sometimes the person who is grieving will not know what help to ask for. They can always request prayers. Both the person being prayed for and the person doing the praying will benefit from this.

9. There are many rituals around the holidays, such as candle lighting services. Many churches offer special religious services. There are other special events held at different times of year by a variety of groups they may want to participate in.

10. Finally, they should be encouraged to pray for themselves. They can set aside time specifically for having a daily devotion. This may involve reading a devotional specifically designed for people in grief, reading passages from the Psalms, and praying.

In the late 1800s, there was a prominent businessman named Horatio. Horatio was a devout Christian. He was a very successful attorney and businessman from Chicago. Horatio and his family had suffered some real tragedies. Horatio and his wife had five lovely children. But two years earlier, their young son had taken very ill and died suddenly, breaking his parent's hearts. It wasn't long after his death that a fire broke out destroying a number of homes along the Lake Michigan shoreline. This included some real estate investments belonging to Horatio.

Horatio and his family decided to take a long vacation in Europe. He had been a big supporter of the famed evangelist Dwight L. Moody, and had become good friends with him. Mr. Moody and his song leader, Ira Sankey were about to hold a large evangelistic campaign in Great Britain and Horatio thought this would be a nice break for his still grieving family. Unfortunately, Horatio had some urgent last minute work he was forced to tend to, so he sent his family on ahead with plans to join them shortly.

Several days after his family left by ship to Europe, Horatio wrapped up his urgent business. He was eager to join his family. He was happily packing for his long trip. A knock came at his door. It was a boy with a telegram from his wife. The cable only had four words, but they were devastating words that would change his life forever. It simply said, "Saved alone, your wife."

The newspapers that day carried the tragic news. It seems the ship his family was on had been struck by another vessel. It had sunk in only twelve short minutes. All four of their daughters had drowned along with more than two hundred other passengers that day. Somehow, his wife had survived. She was waiting for her grief stricken husband in Cardiff, Wales.

I can only imagine how Horatio felt having lost all five of his beloved children. He must have felt an agony in his soul that only someone who has experienced such grief can even begin to understand.

Horatio wrote a letter to a friend. He told how he stayed on the top deck for hour after hour as he made his way by ship to Wales. He watched the rolling waves and wept, grieving the loss of his four precious daughters. At one point, the captain of the ship came out and told Horatio that they were very near to the spot where the tragic collision had occurred.

Horatio looked out over the water where he knew his young innocent daughters had drowned. He says he felt the overwhelming sense of God's presence at that moment, and felt strangely comforted. He was thinking about the redemptive work of Christ on the cross and the promise of His return. Words began to come into his mind, and a poetic verse began taking shape. He wrote the words down that came from his grief during that moment. He asked his friend, who had written many songs, to look over the words and see if music might be put to the words. His friend, Philip Bliss, said that he immediately set to work on the hymn, as he prayed that somehow the hymn would be a source of comfort not only to Horatio and his wife, but others who were grieving. Here are the words to Horatio Spafford's hymn called, "It is well with my Soul".

> When peace, like a river, attendeth my way,
> When sorrows like sea billows roll;
> Whatever my lot, Thou has taught me to say,
> It is well, it is well, with my soul.
>
> o   *Refrain:*
> It is well, with my soul,
> It is well, it is well, with my soul.
>
> Though Satan should buffet, though trials should come,
> this blest assurance control,

That Christ has regarded my helpless estate,
And hath shed His own blood for my soul.

My sin, oh, the bliss of this glorious thought!
My sin, not in part but the whole,
Is nailed to the cross, and I bear it no more,
Praise the Lord, praise the Lord, O my soul!

For me, be it Christ, be it Christ hence to live:
If Jordan above me shall roll,
No pang shall be mine, for in death as in life
Thou wilt whisper Thy peace to my soul.

But, Lord, 'tis for Thee, for Thy coming we wait,
The sky, not the grave, is our goal;
Oh, trump of the angel! Oh, voice of the Lord!
Blessed hope, blessed rest of my soul!

And Lord, haste the day when my faith shall be sight,
The clouds be rolled back as a scroll;
The trump shall resound, and the Lord shall descend,
Even so, it is well with my soul.

    Having a specific plan, or following a step by step guide may or may not be helpful to the person who is grieving. Everyone is a little different, and what works for one may not work for another. The important thing is to be available to the person who is grieving, and encourage them to find the things that work for and help them.
    People tend to fall into routines. Sometimes that is a good thing. However it may be that if a person gets stuck in a routine they will not be able to move forward in their grief journey. It is important to continue making progress and grieving the loss. If a person seems to be stuck, encourage them to try something different. This book is full of suggestions of different things to try.
    Thank you for taking the time to read this resource. My prayer is it will be used to minister to the broken hearted, and those whose spirit has been hurt – who feel like grief has kidnapped their soul. May God use you to minister to them and love them as Christ loved the Church.

God bless you gentle reader.

APPENDIX A

Other Helpful Resources

Clergy Killers: Guidance for Pastors and Congregations Under Attack
By G. Lloyd Rediger
Published by Logos Productions, Inc., 1997

Crying Handbook (The)
By Bob Baugher, Ph.D and Darcie Sims, Ph.D., 2007

Facing Your Giants
By Max Lucado
Published by Thomas Nelson, Inc., 2006

Footsteps Through the Valley
By Darcie D. Sims Ph.D.
Published by Big A and Company, 1993

Gold Country Chaplaincy
PO Box 654
Loomis, CA 95650
916-259-1001
goldcountryadmin@gmail.com

Jesus Calling: Enjoying Peace in His Presence - Devotions for Every Day of the Year
By Sarah Young
Published by Thomas Nelson, 2004

Making Lemonade
Choosing a Positive Pathway After Losing Your Sibling
By Zander Sprague
Published by Paradiso Press, 2008

National Suicide Prevention Hotline
1-800-273-TALK (8255)

Springs in the Valley
By L. B. Cowman
Published by Zondervan, 1997

Streams in the Desert
By L. B. Cowman
Published by Zondervan, 2006

What to Do on the Worst Day of Your Life
By Brian Zahnd
Published by Christian Life, a Strang Company, 2009

When God Weeps
by Joni Eareckson Tada and Steve Estes
Published by Zondervan, 2000

SCRIPTURE REFERENCES

Scripture	Page
Genesis 23	4
Matthew 5:2	4
II Samuel 18:33b	6
Psalm 34:18	20
II Samuel 12:23	21
Psalm 61:1-3	28
Genesis 1:1-2	32
Psalm 6	43
Genesis 2:24	46
Psalm 41:9	48
Hebrews 12:15	54
Romans 5:12	59
Hebrews 13:5	60
Psalm 22:1-2	60
Psalm 22:3-5	61
Luke 12:6-7	64
Galatians 4:6	64
1 Peter 5:7	64
John 3:16	64
Hebrews 4:15-16	65

Reference	Page
Hebrews 6:19-20	65
Psalm 69:1-2	72
Psalm 6:6	72
Psalm 56:8	72
John 13:35	75
Romans 8:28	79
Romans 10:13	79
Ecclesiastes 3:1	79
Hebrews 5:7	86
John 11:35	86
I Samuel 30:1-6	89
I Samuel 30:15	90
I Samuel 17:10	96
Psalm 23	97
John 3:16	102
Romans 3:23	103
John 14:6	103
John 3:16	103
Romans 10:9	104
I John 1:9	104
Psalm 27:4-5	110
II Samuel 1:25	116
II Corinthians 1:3-4	117

About the Author

    Chaplain Terry Morgan is an ordained minister with over 30 years of experience. He has spent 20 years as a law enforcement chaplain. He is the Senior Chaplain/Executive Director of Gold Country Chaplaincy and Press4hope. Morgan is a Master Chaplain Level member of the International Conference of Police Chaplains, and is a member of the International Critical Incident Stress Foundation. He received his Board Certification in Emergency Crisis Response through the American Academy of Experts in Traumatic Stress. Chaplain Morgan has extensive training, and is a certified trainer for QPR suicide prevention, and a provisional trainer for ASIST suicide intervention. He is a member in good standing with the "Assn. of the United States Army" (AUSA). Chaplain Morgan has sat on several boards representing the Faith based Community including the boards of the "Campaign for Community Wellness," and "Advocates for the Mentally Ill Housing". He is currently President of the Board for the Gold Country Veteran Stand Down. Most recently he became a Local Board Member for the Selective Service System Region III.
    Chaplain Morgan was one of a handful of law enforcement chaplains chosen to work with Louisiana Mental Health and the New Orleans Police Dept. immediately following Hurricane Katrina. He has also been one of only a few chaplains selected to work with surviving family members of officers killed in the line of duty during "Police Week" in Washington D.C.
    Chaplain Morgan earned his Masters degree in Ministry in Public Safety, from Trinity Biblical University and his Bachelors degree in Theology from Pacific Coast Bible College. He also has

an Associate of Science Degree in Business Management from Sacramento City College. He has taught Bible college courses, and teaches crisis counseling for chaplains. He is often called upon as an expert in dealing with traumatic stress, and stress management. He has been frequently published in Officer.com magazine on a variety of topics related to law enforcement, and has been featured in "PORAC" magazine and "Extant Magazine". He is the author of the books "The Chaplain's Role, How Clergy Can Work With Law Enforcement", and "Life Celebrations a Guide for Funeral and Memorial Services".

Chaplain Morgan teaches various ministries how to help their own parishioners through critical incidents, crisis, and traumatic events, while exercising good stress management techniques and preventing compassion fatigue or burn out in their ministers.

Rev. Morgan is available for speaking engagements, conferences, and other events. He can be contacted through his website at http://chaplainmorgan.wix.com/chaplainsrole

Other Books by the Author

The Chaplain's Role
How Clergy Can Work With Law Enforcement
This book discusses many general topics surrounding chaplaincy, but it is specifically designed for those working with first responders—more specifically, law enforcement. Within these pages you will find tools you can use to work with law enforcement in a ministry role. This book can be used as a "how to" guide for chaplains. It details out how to really make a difference in your community in times of crisis; and how to come alongside law enforcement in such a way as to be an asset to them.

Life Celebrations
A Guide for Funeral and Memorial Services
Life Celebrations is about people and how to care for them at what may be the worst time of their lives. It shares how to organize and conduct a funeral service from start to finish. The easy to follow step by step directions makes it a great resource. Life Celebrations is crammed full of illustrations and suggestions for putting together an end of life celebration that people will appreciate. The author calls upon his many years of experience conducting funerals for those without a clergy to turn to. "There was a need for a solid resource to turn to when conducting funerals." Said Chaplain Morgan. "I couldn't find a suitable guide, so I decided to write one."

Available in book stores, libraries, Amazon, and on Chaplain Morgan's Website - http://chaplainmorgan.wix.com/chaplainsrole

Made in the USA
San Bernardino, CA
15 April 2015